TOMART's illustrated
DISNEYANA
catalog and price guide
VOLUME THREE

by Tom Tumbusch

Edited by Bob and Claire Raymond

Consultant David R. Smith, Archivist
Walt Disney Productions

Color Photography by Tom Schwartz

TOMART PUBLICATIONS
division of Tomart Corporation
Dayton, Ohio

**To David R. Smith, Archivist,
Paula Sigman, Assistant Archivist, and the Walt Disney Productions
Archives staff, for their role in keeping the genius of Walt Disney alive and
accessible to those who wish to benefit from his many achievements.**

ACKNOWLEDGEMENTS

These books have not been a small undertaking. Many people have helped. Some made major contributions to this extensive DISNEYANA research project. Every bit of information, photocopy, or actual photo helped make the books a little better. I would like to thank these individuals plus the many collectors and dealers who permitted me to photograph their Disneyana items. Special thanks go to Bob Lesser, Harvey and Jan Kamins, Richard Kamins, Ted Hake, Harry Hall, Jim Silva, Bob Coup, John Koukoutsakis, Joe Sarno, Bill Joppeck, Dave and Elaine Hughes, Jerry and Mona Cook, Bruce and Linda Cervon, Donna and Keith Kaonis, Bernie Shine, Morris Hamasaki, Phil Ellis and Carol, Ed and Elaine Levin, Bob Molinari, Don and Dee Toms, Evie Wilson, Jean Toll, Charles Sexton, Karl Price, Stan Pawlowski, Kim and Julie McEuen, Ray Walsh, Dennis Mathiason, Roger Le Roque, Nick Farago, Greg Shelton, George McIntyre, Von Crabill and George Hagenauer for their help ... and to Virginia Gann for caring so many years for her Borgfeldt ducks.

For their moral support and guidance outside the field of Disneyana I am deeply indebted to Stan Freedman, Marilyn Scott, Pete Trohatos, Kirk Febus, Dave Gross, George Might, Karen Morgan, and Rebecca Trissel.

My daughter Amy provided assistance in many ways, particularly in assembling and filing the thousands of bits of data, plus assistance in photographing her stuffed characters and dolls, and help with the final artwork.

A special thanks also to Rick Lenhard and his crew at Boldruler Typesetters for excellent service and cooperation in providing the typography. Central Printing in Dayton and Carpenter Lithographers in Springfield, Ohio printed the three volumes. Production help thanks are also in order for Tom Vukovic and his staff at CompuColor and to Brock Hull at Hull Paper Co.

Everyone who enjoys the 60 pages of color photography in the three volumes can thank Tom Schwartz and his assistant, Fred Boomer, for over six months of work setting up and photographing all the items shown in color.

And to the editors — collectors Bob and Claire Raymond, and Dave Smith, Archivist, Walt Disney Productions and Paula Sigman, Assistant Archivist — for all the time they spent reviewing, correcting, and otherwise improving the manuscript, I extend my personal gratitude.

Lastly it's a proud father who thanks his 16 year old son, Thomas N., for entering everything into an Atari 800 computer, for many rewrites, and a large part of the typesetting job. We stuck it out together.

Tom Tumbusch
November, 1985

The Tomart Illustrated DISNEYANA Catalog and Price Guide will be updated on a regular basis. If you wish to be notified when the supplements become available, send a self-addressed stamped envelope to Tomart Publications, P. O. Box 2102, Dayton, OH 45429.

Mickey Nearly Swamped by Fan Mail

Mickey Mouse *Registering Enthusiasm Over His Fan Mail*

2—Two Col. Scene (Mat 10c; Cut 50c)

All records for fan mail by a cinematic star anywhere are believed to have been broken by Hollywood's tiniest celebrity, Mickey Mouse, with more than 20,000 letters pouring into the Walt Disney Studios in the brief interval of three weeks. It was necessary to deliver Mickey's mail in trucks to the studio and engage a special corps of office assistants to sort it.

It all came about through the publication of a comic strip showing Mickey having his picture taken for his fans, which was syndicated nationally. Immediately following publication of the strip cartoon in the newspapers, the deluge of fan mail started pouring into Hollywood.

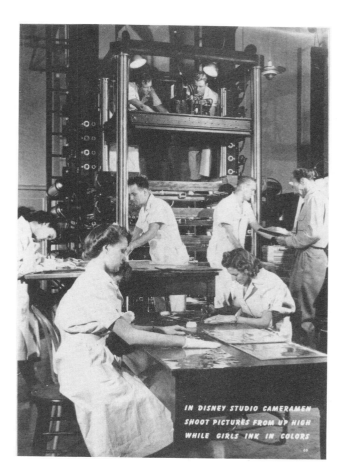

IN DISNEY STUDIO CAMERAMEN SHOOT PICTURES FROM UP HIGH WHILE GIRLS INK IN COLORS

In Volume One of *Tomart's Illustrated DISNEYANA Catalog and Price Guide* information on all facets of Disneyana collecting was presented. Material included the growth of the hobby and the recognition of Disneyana as a popular culture art form. There was also an expanded explanation on how to use this three volume series, the values presented, and the many guidelines on how collectors can locate and obtain items of Disneyana.

The Disney Time Line covered the years 1915 to 1940 in Volume One ... the period from Walt Disney's first art lesson in Chicago up through Fantasia, his third animated feature. Volume Two covered the ten year span from the second World War, when the studio diverted from its growth plans to support the war effort, until business returned to "normal" with the release of Cinderella in 1950.

Throughout both previous volumes, illustrations have been used to show how and when characters have changed. This background will be helpful to the reader in identifying items not shown in these volumes. Historical data useful in making a more positive identification has also been included.

The Disney Time Line continues now as Walt Disney was planning how the studio might become more involved in a new sensation called television ... and a new amusement park concept called Disneyland.

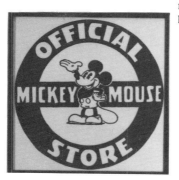

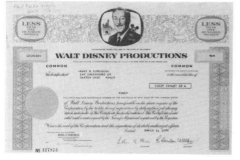

Fan card for **Alice In Wonderland.**

1951

The animated *Alice In Wonderland* (July 28) was a disappointment at the box office and thus produced a smaller amount of character merchandise. *Nature's Half Acre* became the third True-Life Adventure to win an Oscar, and 18 new cartoons were released. Occupied Japan marks were revised to "Made in Japan". Walt Disney hosted his second Christmas TV special entitled "The Walt Disney Christmas Show".

1952

The Story of Robin Hood (June 26) was the second feature made in England . . . one that inspired a good variety of books and merchandise. Walt fell short of his goal of one new animated feature each year, but some memorable cartoons resulted: *Donald Applecore; Lambert, The Sheepish Lion; Trick or Treat* and *Pluto's Christmas Tree*. *Water Birds* was an Academy Award winner, the fourth year running a True-Life Adventure won the honor.

Walt continued to resist tempting TV offers, as plans for a theme park were taking shape.

(Above) Press book photo from **Alice In Wonderland.** *A similar press book photo from* **20,000 Leagues Under the Sea** *(Right).*

1953

Peter Pan, Disney's best sight gag feature, premiered Feb 5, generating more merchandise than *Cinderella*. *Bear Country* continued the string of True-Life Academy Award winners. There were more winners as well — *The Alaskan Eskimo,* the first "People and Places" film, and *Toot, Whistle, Plunk, and Boom,* Disney's first Cinemascope cartoon. *The Simple Things* was the last Mickey Mouse theatrical cartoon short. *Melody (Adventures in Music)* was the first 3-D cartoon, followed by another later in the year with Donald in *Working for Peanuts. Ben and Me* was the year's best animated featurette.

The Sword and the Rose (July 23), and another British product, *Rob Roy the Highland Rogue,* was the last feature released by RKO. *The Living Desert* (Nov 10) was the first product released by Disney's new Buena Vista Distribution Company, and it too won an Academy Award.

Peter Pan *fan card.*

1954

Features of note were *Rob Roy the Highland Rogue* (Feb 4), *The Vanishing Prairie* (Aug 17), and *20,000 Leagues Under the Sea* (Dec 23), the first Disney film use of elaborate special

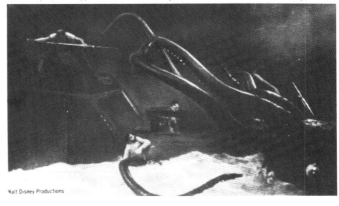

effects. Cartoons and animated segments of 40's composite movies were being re-released to supply a large portion of the declining cartoon market. *Pigs Is Pigs* and Donald in *Grand Canyonscope* led the list of new entries.

The big event of the year was the first weekly TV contract. All three networks had been after Walt to air his cartoon classics on TV. Disney finally agreed to a different idea. He and Roy were risking everything they had to build Disneyland. Walt wanted to do a TV show for promotional purposes. The program was first called *Disneyland* and the first show, "The Disneyland Story". This and succeeding "progress reports" took the viewer behind the scenes and made them feel part of Disneyland's planning and construction process. Millions became involved and Disneyland was a global phenomenon before opening day. Opening day (7/17/55) was the occasion for a live spectacular on ABC-TV.

Disneyland pre-opening postcard #1 showing Walt Disney describing an aerial plan of the park.

The first season was a smash in every respect. A great deal of the programming came from Disney's existing library. The made for TV *Davy Crockett, Indian Fighter* (Dec 15), starring Fess Parker and Buddy Ebsen, triggered a gigantic fad. The next two shows in the trilogy — *Davy Crockett Goes to Congress* (1/26/55) and *Davy Crockett at the Alamo* (2/23/55) — are classic examples of Disney's story telling genius. His family programming truly entertained everyone in the family — not just the kids.

1955

The year proved to be a major milestone for Walt Disney Productions and an important one in the history of Disneyana. Once it was the generally accepted dividing year between items that were collectible and those that were not. Today, events of 1955 are the subject of some specialized areas of collecting.

Lady and the Tramp premiered in June and the Disneyland theme park opened in July. Davy Crockett had become the biggest hero since Hopalong Cassidy. The TV *Mickey Mouse Club* began as an hour show on Oct 3, airing each Monday thru Friday in most parts of the country from 5:00 to 6:00 pm.

Prior to *Lady and the Tramp*, merchandise wasn't normally available until 5 or 6 months after a film's release. O.B.Johnston, the head of the Character Merchandising Division since it was formed, instituted a new policy. Manufacturers were pre-licensed in time to have merchandise available for the film's release date. The idea worked. Publicity was enhanced, more manufacturers participated, and products were available when most filmgoers wanted them — soon after seeing the film. *Lady* animation cels are more widely distributed than those of other features. Great quantities were mounted, priced under $5 and sold at Disneyland's Art Corner so anyone could own Disney original art.

Disneyland opened July 17, representing an initial investment of $17 million. Originally, there were 22 major attractions, divided in five themed lands — Main Street USA, Adventureland, Frontierland, Fantasyland, and Tomorrowland. The pre-sell job on TV, plus spectacular fulfillment on the promise of a special "Magic Kingdom" made Disneyland a "must" for worker and world leader alike. The constantly changing maps, postcards, guidebooks, buttons, and souvenirs have become popular Disneyana. Disneyland never stops growing, and there is always some special event being commemorated throughout the park and on merchandise.

The Mickey Mouse Club pumped new life into the title character as he reached a new generation of children. They found him just as delightful as their parents had in the 30's. The result was a new wave of Mickey merchandise hallmarked by the club emblem. This time around there were also Mousekete-

eers — a cast of talented kids and two adult leaders. Monday was "Fun With Music Day". Tuesday: "Guest Star Day". Wednesday: "Anything Can Happen Day". Thursday: "Circus Day". Friday: "Talent Roundup Day". The format also included cartoons, science, a variety of educational and "what I want to be" sequences, plus teen adventure serials such as "The Hardy Boys" and "Spin and Marty". Thousands of merchandise items, many untraditionally Disney, were connected with the club. There were 38 licensed manufacturers the first year. The program was reduced to a half-hour in the fourth year, and went into off-network syndication in 1962.

There were more re-released cartoons than new ones, most of which were being made in Cinemascope in an attempt to save a dying market. *Men Against the Arctic,* a People and Places short, won an Academy Award. Donald's *No Hunting* was nominated. *The African Lion* was released in October, *The Littlest Outlaw* in December.

1956

The last series of theatrical cartoon shorts made by Walt Disney ended with: *Chips Ahoy, Hooked Bear,* and *In the Bag.* That part of the business was dead. It was the age of TV and Disneyland.

Davy Crockett and the River Pirates (July 18) was the most popular release of the year even though it had already appeared on TV. *Secrets of Life* (Nov 20), likely the most inventive of the True-Life Adventure feature documentaries, opened the viewer's eyes to natural phenomena impossible to see without the advances in camera technology developed in conjunction with the film.

Disneyland's expansion included the addition of Tom Sawyer's Island, Storybook Land, Rainbow Caverns, and the Skyway between Tomorrowland and Fantasyland.

1957

Our Friend The Atom appeared Jan 23 on the Disneyland TV show and was released theatrically in Europe. It explained atomic energy in laymen's terms.

The *Andy Burnett* series began Oct 2 and was the subject of six adventures in the 57-58 TV season. The TV smash of the

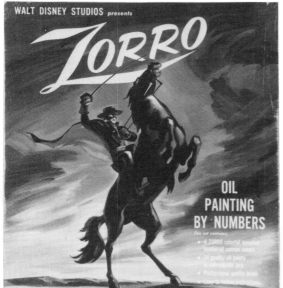

year was the *Zorro* program that began as a weekly half hour series in the fall and ran two years.

Disneyland opened the Sleeping Beauty Castle exhibit, Midget Autopia, and the Viewliner (since replaced by the monorail system).

Perri (Aug 28) was a popular True-Life Fantasy theatrical

feature. *Old Yeller* was released in December. Non-animated shorts: *The Wetback Hound,* and *Niok,* as well as the animated *Mars and Beyond* received acclaim.

Walt Disney was presented with the 25th million Mickey Mouse watch produced.

1958

The *Disneyland* TV series was retitled *Walt Disney Presents. The Nine Lives of Elfego Baca* and *Tales of Texas John Slaughter* first appeared. Each was the subject of many TV episodes into the early 60's. *The White Wilderness* True-Life Adventure feature was released in August. *Tonka* followed in December.

Big things were taking shape at Disneyland. The sailing ship Columbia, the Grand Canyon Diorama, Alice in Wonderland, and the excursion train were added.

1959

The long awaited $6 million animated feature, *Sleeping Beauty,* arrived Jan 29, the first to be made in 70mm Techni-

Souvenir program for **Sleeping Beauty.**

rama. Public response was disappointing and the film only barely covered its production cost. Fortunately, *The Shaggy Dog* (Mar 19), produced for just over a million, grossed over $10 million in film rentals. *Darby O'Gill and the Little People* was released in June.

The weekly TV series generated *The Birth of the Swamp Fox* (Oct 23), and the Revolutionary War hero became the subject of many TV episodes and appeared on some merchandise. *Grand Canyon* won an Oscar and *Mysteries of the Deep* was the year's nature film candidate.

The biggest expansion since Disneyland's opening included the addition of the Submarine Voyage, the Disneyland-Alweg Monorail system, the 14 story high Matterhorn Mountain bobsled run, two replacement Autopia Freeways, the enlargement of the Motorboat Cruise and Super Autopias in Tomorrowland.

1960

Notable feature films of the year were *Toby Tyler* (Jan), *Kidnapped* (Feb), *The Sign of Zorro* (June), *Pollyanna* (May) and *Swiss Family Robinson* (Dec). Zorro also returned to appear on the weekly TV show. *El Bandito* (Oct 30) was the first such special.

Disneyland added Nature's Wonderland, inspired by the True-Life Adventures. Over 200 animals, birds, and reptiles were viewed, in a re-creation of wilderness and desert regions, from Western mine trains. (Since replaced by Big Thunder Mountain Railroad.)

The demand for Mickey Mouse watches reached a new low. No new watches with Mickey's picture were produced until 1967, only ones with the words Mickey Mouse.

1961

101 Dalmatians (Jan 25) was the first animated feature to fully utilize a special Xerox camera developed by Ub Iwerks. It eliminated the need for inking the animator's line drawing onto the cel by substituting an electrostatic transfer from the animation art. This gave the characters a softer look. The process was used for over 20 years.

The Absent-Minded Professor (Mar 16) introduced the world to "flubber". The huge success of the film resulted in take-offs and sequels produced in later years. *The Parent Trap* was released in June and *Babes In Toyland* was the Christmas film.

The weekly TV program moved to the NBC network in the fall. The program was re-named *Walt Disney's Wonderful World of Color*. Ludwig Von Drake, a new animated character, was introduced and went on to host many Disney network TV shows. *Hans Brinker, or The Silver Skates, The Prince and the Pauper,* and *Disneyland After Dark* were standouts in the first season of color programs.

Additions to Disneyland included expansion of the Monorail system to the Disneyland Hotel and the Flying Saucer ride in Tomorrowland (since removed). The first Grad Night was held.

1962

The major films were: *Moon Pilot, Bon Voyage, Big Red, Almost Angels, The Legend of Lobo,* and *In Search of the Castaways.* A telltale pattern was setting in at the Studio. The emphasis was being put on production rather than the unique quality that made the Studio world renowned. Formula, for a large part, had replaced experimentation and risk-taking. Few features during this period produced Disneyana other than pressbooks and film promotional material. Since this is of little interest to collectors, only live action features that were merchandised will continue to be mentioned. One test for future stories under consideration might be "how can it be merchandised"? Merchandise potential can provide a good indication on how involved a viewer could get in the story. And without a good level of involvement, how good could the finished film be?

The focus of the company was on Disneyland. *The Golden Horseshoe Revue,* a story built around the theme park attraction, premiered the fall TV season — and was released theatrically in Europe. It was also the year when too many programs featured animals as heroes. Each was well done, but still there was a feeling you saw it all before.

The Jungle Cruise was enlarged at Disneyland. The Swiss Family Treehouse, the Plaza Pavilion Restaurant, and Tahitian Terrace were added.

1963

Mechanical robotics were used in the original Jungle Cruise back in the 50's. However, the Lincoln exhibit being prepared for the New York World Fair required something more. The result was "Audio-Animatronics", a sophisticated system that creates life-like movements in robot animals and humans — down to the blink of an eye. The technique was also the basis of the Enchanted Tiki Room, Disneyland's major addition for the year.

Son of Flubber (Jan), *Savage Sam* (Aug), and *Sword in the Stone* (Dec) were reflected in character merchandise.

1964

Disney was a big participant in the 1964-65 New York World's Fair. The company had developed several exhibits: "It's a Small World" for Pepsi Cola/UNICEF, "Great Moments with Mr. Lincoln" for the State of Illinois, the "Carousel of Progress" for GE, and, "Primeval World" for Ford.

The Misadventures of Merlin Jones (Jan) and *Emil and the Detectives* (Dec) resulted in books, but *Mary Poppins* (Aug 29) was the subject of the biggest merchandise bonanza since *Lady and the Tramp. The Scarecrow of Romney Marsh* (Feb 9) and several episodes of *Gallegher,* a teenage detective, highlighted TV events of the year.

The Postmaster General announced the zip code on Apr 30

be transplanted to the park. Slightly over 43 square miles of land in central Florida had been secretly pieced together in preparation of the announcement of Walt Disney World in November.

The Sunday night TV show had developed a regular mix of theatrical live-action films, animal as hero episodes, made TV adventure shows and cartoon anthologies. *That Darn Cat* (Dec), a live action feature, resulted in books and a few promotional items.

Movie program from Mary Poppins *and movie still for* Son of Flubber.

to be effective July 1. Compliance was excellent and zip codes appear in the manufacturer's addresses found on original boxes of items produced subsequent to the effective date.

Major construction was underway at Disneyland but the only new offering was "Below Decks", the living and working quarters on the Columbia, the replica of the first ship to sail around the world.

1965

Disneyland marked its 10th anniversary and Great Moments with Mr. Lincoln became the first World's Fair exhibit to

1966

Winnie the Pooh and the Honey Tree (Feb) was released as a featurette. Walt Disney World planning was a genuine news event whenever new ideas surfaced or there was a hint when construction might begin. Disneyland opened New Orleans Square, It's A Small World, and Primeval World.

The impact of the death of Walt Disney on Dec 15 was one of world leader magnitude. He was really a simple man who sought only to do the things he liked to do. Each project was a chance to do things differently and better than before. Excellence was the only acceptable option. His motivation was never money or power. Disney's fertile imagination could envision dreams in great detail. His greatest assets were storytelling and his ability to extend himself through others who complemented his ideas and did much of the actual work. His real reward was seeing his dreams come true. Disney's sense of history and public relations were exceeded only by his knack of knowing what to do when things went wrong. The fellow who said: "Nice guys finish last" never knew Walt Disney.

Walt Disney announced the location of the New York World's Fair Primeval World exhibit at Disneyland, and soon thereafter, a new vacation theme park to be built in Florida.

Walter Elias Disney
Dec 5, 1901 — Dec 15, 1966.

8

1967

Work on Walt Disney World, soon the largest private construction project in America, began on May 30.

Feature films included *The Adventures of Bullwhip Griffin* (March), *The Gnome-Mobile* (July), and *The Happiest Millionaire* (June). *The Jungle Book,* Disney's 19th animated feature premiered on Oct 18.

Movie still for **The Jungle Book***.*

Pirates of the Caribbean and a completely new Tomorrowland opened at Disneyland. Included were the People-Mover, G.E. Carousel of Progress (since moved to Walt Disney World), Adventures Thru Inner Space, Flight to the Moon, Rocket Jets, Tomorrowland Terrace and the 360 Circlevision version of *America the Beautiful*.

Character watches with Mickey's picture resumed production for the first time since 1960.

1968

A nostalgia boom had been building since 1966. Classic pie-eyed Mickeys and Minnies were appearing on a growing variety of unauthorized merchandise. Joining the trend, the company agreed to license old style characters. They have appeared on new merchandise ever since.

Winnie the Pooh and the Blustery Day was released Dec 20.

1969

The Love Bug (Mar) introduced Herbie the VW and was a surprise box office winner.

The engineering masterpiece of Disneyland, The Haunted Mansion, began operation. The name of the Sunday TV program was changed again: from *Walt Disney's Wonderful World of Color* to *The Wonderful World of Disney*.

1970

The Walt Disney Archives was established June 22.

The Aristocats, the last animated feature in which Walt Disney was involved, premiered on Dec 24.

1971

Walt Disney World opened on Oct 1 at an initial cost of $400 million. Roy O. Disney was on hand to dedicate the "Vacation Kingdom", but died soon after on Dec 20. He was president of Walt Disney Productions from 1945 to 1968, chairman and CEO until his death. He was a quiet man largely responsible for making Walt's dreams come true.

Bob Hope hosted a TV special opening "the Florida Project". In addition to the theme park, there were hotels, golfing, swimming, tennis, horseback riding, boating, and convention

facilities. Not all the attractions from Disneyland were duplicated at Walt Disney World, but the Florida park opened with some new ones: The Country Bear Jamboree and The Mickey Mouse Revue (since removed to Tokyo Disneyland). The centerpiece was Cinderella Castle.

The Walt Disney Distributing Company was formed, and operated from Lake Buena Vista on the Walt Disney World property. The company sold Disney character merchandise of its own design and an extensive catalog of giftware. Items sold outside the theme parks were marketed under the label of

"Disney Gifts". The company published merchandise catalogs from 1971 to 1977 when the operation was dissolved.

Bedknobs and Broomsticks was released Dec 13.

©W.D.P., a copyright form widely used in the 40's and 50's, was specifically eliminated from the company's official copyright practices.

1972-1980

The first known attempt to organize a Disneyana Collectors Club was made by Stephen Horn in 1972. Members received a membership card, homemade button, and a ditto newsletter.

Walt Disney Productions celebrated its 50th anniversary in 1973 with a series of events that concluded with the November release of the animated version of *Robin Hood*.

DISNEYANA by Cecil Munsey was published by Hawthorn Books in 1974. Pirates of the Caribbean was the first major attraction added to Walt Disney World. America Sings was added to Disneyland, replacing the Carousel of Progress, which was moved to Walt Disney World.

The Space Mountain attraction opened Jan 1975 at Walt Disney World. Disneyland got the simulated space ride in 1977. In June 1975, America on Parade, commemorating the 200th birthday of the United States, began in both theme parks. It was the broadest merchandised event the theme parks had ever produced. The elaborate show parade continued until September 1976.

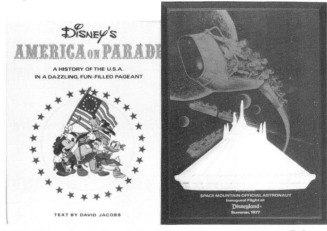

Official America On Parade book (left) and press giveaway wall plaque commemorating the opening of the Space Mountain attraction at Disneyland (right).

The Disneyana Shop in the Disneyland Emporium complex opened in Jan 1976. Originally, the shop sold antique Disneyana items purchased at toy shows and from private dealers. Each item was authenticated and sold with a description card. Maintaining a steady supply of merchandise, however, was impossible. Within three years, the shop converted completely to limited edition collectibles, cels, and other items of a collectible nature.

In Jan 1977, a new TV Mickey Mouse Club went on the air. It failed to attract interest equal to the old black and white episodes being syndicated at the time. It didn't last two full seasons. *The Rescuers* (Jun) and *Pete's Dragon* (Nov) were 77's best merchandised features.

The big event of 1978 was Mickey Mouse's 50th birthday, celebrated the year long at Disneyland, Walt Disney World,

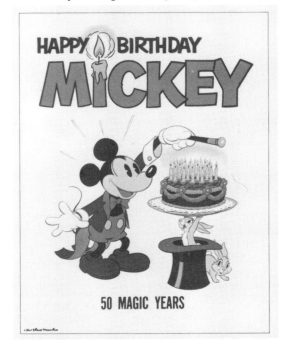

(Above) May Co. fan card issued for Mickey's 50th Birthday contest and (below) the Mickey's Mouse star installed in front of the Mann Chinese Theater along the Hollywood Blvd. "Walk of the Stars" (1978).

and in a special release of *Mickey's Birthday Party* at theaters across the nation. Big Thunder Mountain Railroad opened Sept 1978 at Disneyland and two years later at Walt Disney World. *The Black Hole* was released Dec 21, 1979.

The Mouse Club, a group of Disneyana collectors, was organized and issued its first newsletter in January, 1980. Disneyland was 25 years old in 1980. After 20 years on NBC *The Wonderful World of Disney* was cancelled. CBS picked up the program, but the arrangement concluded with the 1982 season, ending a 27-year institution.

1981-1985

Walt Disney World had its tencennial in 1981. EPCOT Center opened Oct 1, 1982 at an initial cost exceeding $1 billion. *The Fox and the Hound* premiered in July, 1981.

The first Mouse Club convention was held in Anaheim, CA in Aug 1982. The second a year later. The annual convention was skipped in '84 due to the Olympics, but resumed in 1985.

TRON (July '82) was designed in tune with the electronic game craze. April 15, 1983 was the official opening day of Tokyo Disneyland. The Disney Channel, a pay-TV service,

began broadcasting in April. "Horizons" was added to EPCOT and a new Fantasyland greeted June visitors to the original Disneyland (The Pirate Ship, Skull Rock and a movie theater were removed to make room). The year ended with the release of *Mickey's Christmas Carol,* the first new Mickey short in 30 years.

Donald's 50th birthday was the major event of 1984 until the Olympics took over in July and August. Back in 1980, Disney artist Bob Moore designed Sam the Eagle, the mascot for the Olympics, and Walt Disney Productions donated him to the Los Angeles Olympic Committee. Sam appeared on thousands of items and promotional material in the four year period. Sport Goofy, the official mascot of the French Olympic team, was also widely merchandised.

Disney's feature films had been going downhill for several years. The film business and audiences changed while Disney continued to turn out "G" rated family entertainment. Older teens and young adults (the majority of movie audiences) preferred "PG" and "R" rated films. Even top Disney animated features caused problems for exhibitors. The films would do well in day and evening showings — the child and family market — but did poorly for showings after 8:45 pm. The Disney name on a film, long an asset, became a liability to the movie house and a turn-off to many filmgoers. Thus Touchstone Films was formed. *Splash* was the first release in Mar 1984.

Disneyland marked its 30th year in 1985 with a prize awarded to every 30th, 300th, 3,000th, 300,000th and 3 millionth visitor. An estimated $12 million dollars worth of gifts and GM automobiles were awarded to attract visitors — over two thirds the amount needed to construct the original Disneyland 30 years previous.

The Black Cauldron (July) was the first animated feature in which the Xerox camera was replaced by a new photo transfer system that restored the hand-inked look of earlier animation.

The company survived two takeover attempts in 1984 and attracted new management. They appear to have returned the Studio to solid ground. Charting the future of the *Disney Time Line* is in their hands. It promises to be an exciting time for Walt Disney Productions and for the collection of Disneyana.

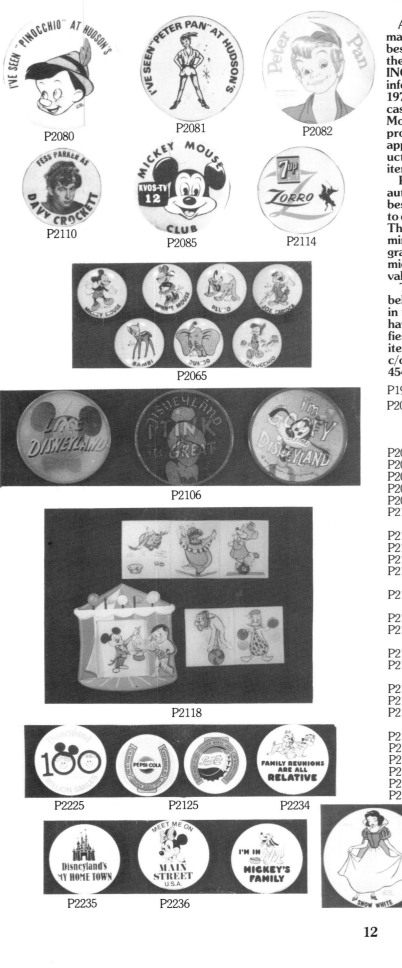

P2080

P2081

P2082

P2110

P2085

P2114

P2065

P2106

P2118

P2225

P2125

P2234

P2235

P2236

IMPORTANT PRICE and DATE INFORMATION
for VOLUME THREE

At each classification there is a brief overview of the material covered, followed by item listings. Included is the best information currently available on manufacturers and the years licensed. THIS INFORMATION IS NOT ALL-INCLUSIVE AND ERRORS UNDOUBTEDLY EXIST. The information is most reliable for the years 1934-50 and from 1970 to 1984, although it might not be precise. In some cases the possible error is the listing of a year not licensed. More often it will be the absence of a year in which Disney products were made. In some cases a manufacturer's name appears under a classification even though none of its products are listed. The licensing records are sound, but the items have yet to be located and cataloged by the author.

Price range estimates are based on the experience of the author. In cases where sufficient trade experience is absent, best guesstimates are provided. Where a price range refers to different size items, the high end refers to the largest size. The greater the price spread, the more valuable a strictly mint item. Also, in the case of a wide price range, "fine" grade items are worth substantially less than the average or mid-price shown. If the price range shown is 10-100, the fine value is around 40 not 50 to 55.

This sometimes flawed information is provided in the belief that available data will lead to improved scholarship in the future. Any collectors or former Disney employees having printed data or dated Disneyana material that clarifies this information are encouraged to send photos of items or photocopies of printed material to Tom Tumbusch c/o Tomart Publications, P.O. Box 2102, Dayton, Ohio 45429.

P1900 PINBACK BUTTONS, BADGES & TABS continued

P2065	Donald Duck Peanut Butter (10 different — Mickey, Minnie, Donald, Pluto, Snow White, Dopey, Pinocchio, Dumbo, Bambi and Joe Carioca, each	5 - 25
P2080	Pinocchio at Hudson's	10 - 35
P2081	Peter Pan at Hudson's	10 - 35
P2082	Peter Pan 3"	3 - 10
P2085	Mickey Mouse Club (KVOS-TV 12)	8 - 24
P2086	TV Mickey Mouse Club buttons and tabs	1 - 12
P2106	Disneyland flasher badges, Mickey, Goofy or Tinker Bell, each	2 - 10
P2109	Donald Disneyland flasher badge	5 - 30
P2110	Fess Parker as Davy Crockett	5 - 30
P2114	Zorro (7up) 1957	1 - 7
P2115	Disneyland yearly anniversery pins (plastic or metal) 1956 to date, each	2-35
P2118	Cheerios Wiggle Picture badge and 6 inserts (1957)	8 - 80
P2125	Golden Horseshoe Revue (2 versions), each	4 - 25
P2128	Mod Mickey or Minnie's Yoo Hoo (unauthorized), each	3 - 18
P2135	Character theme park souvenir 3" buttons, each	1 - 6
P2140	Walt Disney World yearly anniversary pins (plastic) 1972 to date, each	1 - 25
P2145	Disney On Parade	2 - 12
P2150	50 Happy Years (1973)	3 - 15
P2151	Fort Wilderness Campground Resort w/Mickey (1973)	1 - 8
P2152	I've Had Fun With Music	1 - 5
P2155	I Like Walt Disney Music	1 - 5
P2156	Liberty Square Medal	5 - 15
P2160	'74 Grad Nite	4 - 20
P2165	Disneyland Grad Nite '75 or '76, each	3 - 15
P2166	Snow White or any 7 Dwarf	

P2166

P2160   P2165

P2150   P2145   P2280

P2128

P2601   P2600   P2604   P2606

P2170

P2476   P2480

P2500

P2174   P2175

P2135   P2870

P2820

P2821

P2232 P2233 P2230

P2204 P2229

P2152 P2582 P2208 P2578 P2575 P2577 P2576

P2155 P2475 P2206

P2707

P2715 P2712

P2705 P2701 P2700 P2706

P2703

P2145

P2405 P2400 P2410 P2411

P2515 P2516 P2510

P2502 P2501 P2509

P2470 P2208 P2140

P2895 P2579 P2850

14

	(Benay-Albee) 1975, each	1 - 7
	America on Parade (See A4030)	
P2168	Mother's Day 1978	2 - 10
P2169	Orange Bird tab	1 - 5
P2170	Disneyland Grad Nite '77, '78, '79, or '80	1 - 10
P2174	Disneyland Grad Nite '81, '82, '83, '84 or '85	1 - 5
P2175	Walt Disney World Grad Nite '84 or '85	1 - 5
P2190	"A Different Glass Each Week"	2 - 10
P2203	Cake Happy Birthday Mickey, Disneyland or Walt Disney World, each	1 - 10
P2204	I grew up on Mickey Mouse	1 - 3
P2205	Mickey's Month 1982 or '84, each	1 - 5
P2206	Happy Birthday Mickey — phone	.50 - 1
P2208	Happy Birthday Mickey — 56 years	2 - 12
P2225	Disneyland 100 Million Smiles	5 - 25
P2226	Disneyland 200 Million	1 - 10
P2229	Disneyland 25 (Silver) 1"	1 - 8
P2230	Disneyland 25 Mickey or Minnie, each	5 - 10
P2232	I Was There — Disneyland 25th Birthday Party	1 - 8
P2233	I'm 25 Today Too!	2 - 12
P2234	Family Reunions are all RELATIVE	2 - 12
P2235	Disneyland's My Home Town	2 - 12
P2237	Disneyland Anniversary buttons 26th thru 29th year, each	1 - 5
P2241	Disneyland 30th Year souvenir button	.50 - 1
P2242	30th — And the Best Has Yet To Come, 2" or 3", each	1 - 3
P2243	30th — I'm A Winner	1 - 4
P2244	30th — Cast Member	1 - 5
P2245	30th — Official Birthday Party button	1 - 2
P2246	30th — Sword in the Stone	1 - 5
P2247	30th — Parade button	2 - 12
P2248	30th — Cloisonne lapel button	2 - 15
P2249	30th — Hollywood Bowl Concert	1 - 5
P2279	Tencennial Press Club	5 - 25
P2280	Walt Disney World — Tencennial	1 - 5
P2400	Space Mountain (4 versions), each	2 - 10
P2405	Big Thunder Mountain Railroad	2 - 10
P2410	New Fantasyland — May 1983	2 - 10
P2411	New Fantasyland — Sword in the Stone	3 - 15

Costuming Division Cast Buttons Walt Disney World (P2450-P2455)

P2450	Maleficent — You Want What Size!	25 - 75
P2451	Happiness is a New Spring Wardrobe!	25 - 75
P2452	Smile! It's a Nice Reflection on You! (round)	25 - 75
P2453	When You're Lookin' Good, We're Lookin' Good!	25 - 75
P2454	Wardrobe Gets My Vote!	20 - 60
P2455	Snow White — Season's Greetings 3D button	15 - 45
	EPCOT Buttons (see E6079-E6113)	
P2470	Salute to Georgia, Walt Disney World	1 - 10
P2471	Salute to Canada, Walt Disney World	1 - 10
P2475	WED and MAPO OPEN HOUSE	1 - 10
P2476	Festival Japan '80, '81 or '82, each	1 - 3
P2480	Festival Mexico	1 - 3
P2481	Saludos Puerto Rico (WOW)	1 - 3
P2490	Thumper Easter Egg Hunt 1983 or 1984	1 - 3
P2500	Disneyland Celebrates America	1 - 5
P2501	Sport Goofy	1 - 3
P2502	Sport Goofy set of 4	5 - 15
P2509	The Sport Goofy Trophy — Walt Disney World	2 - 12
P2510	20th Anniversary of New York World's Fair	1 - 5
P2515	Disneyland convention button (round or oval)	1 - 2
P2516	Disneyland convention name tag	1 - 2
P2517	Ask Me About buttons in shape of Mickey Mouse (many different) promoting events of features of Walt Disney World, each	2 - 18
	Tokyo Disneyland buttons (See T5000)	
P2540	Tour World Showcase Time Trials	2 - 10
P2575	Aspen Fantasia — Winterland '83	1 - 10
P2576	Walt Disney Home Video	2 - 12
P2577	Find It in the Library Media Center	1 - 8
P2578	Mickey's Knights	1 - 5
P2579	Magic Kingdom Club, Donald	2 - 12
P2580	Magic Kingdom Club, Mickey	1 - 5
P2582	Donald — I'm a Fire Safety Expert	1 - 10

P2205   P2451   P2454   P2455   P2453

P2825

15

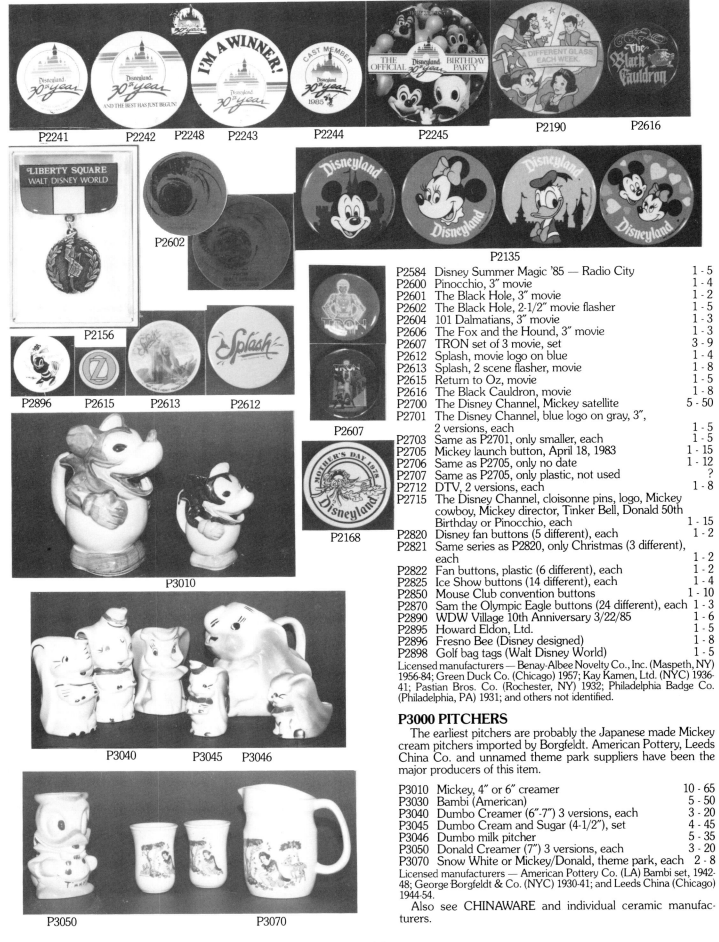

P2241　P2242　P2248　P2243　P2244　P2245　P2190　P2616

P2602

P2156

P2135

P2896　P2615　P2613　P2612

P2607

P2168

P3010

P3040　P3045　P3046

P3050　P3070

P2584	Disney Summer Magic '85 — Radio City	1 - 5
P2600	Pinocchio, 3″ movie	1 - 4
P2601	The Black Hole, 3″ movie	1 - 2
P2602	The Black Hole, 2-1/2″ movie flasher	1 - 5
P2604	101 Dalmatians, 3″ movie	1 - 3
P2606	The Fox and the Hound, 3″ movie	1 - 3
P2607	TRON set of 3 movie, set	3 - 9
P2612	Splash, movie logo on blue	1 - 4
P2613	Splash, 2 scene flasher, movie	1 - 8
P2615	Return to Oz, movie	1 - 5
P2616	The Black Cauldron, movie	1 - 8
P2700	The Disney Channel, Mickey satellite	5 - 50
P2701	The Disney Channel, blue logo on gray, 3″, 2 versions, each	1 - 5
P2703	Same as P2701, only smaller, each	1 - 5
P2705	Mickey launch button, April 18, 1983	1 - 15
P2706	Same as P2705, only no date	1 - 12
P2707	Same as P2705, only plastic, not used	?
P2712	DTV, 2 versions, each	1 - 8
P2715	The Disney Channel, cloisonne pins, logo, Mickey cowboy, Mickey director, Tinker Bell, Donald 50th Birthday or Pinocchio, each	1 - 15
P2820	Disney fan buttons (5 different), each	1 - 2
P2821	Same series as P2820, only Christmas (3 different), each	1 - 2
P2822	Fan buttons, plastic (6 different), each	1 - 2
P2825	Ice Show buttons (14 different), each	1 - 4
P2850	Mouse Club convention buttons	1 - 10
P2870	Sam the Olympic Eagle buttons (24 different), each	1 - 3
P2890	WDW Village 10th Anniversary 3/22/85	1 - 6
P2895	Howard Eldon, Ltd.	1 - 5
P2896	Fresno Bee (Disney designed)	1 - 8
P2898	Golf bag tags (Walt Disney World)	1 - 5

Licensed manufacturers — Benay-Albee Novelty Co., Inc. (Maspeth, NY) 1956-84; Green Duck Co. (Chicago) 1957; Kay Kamen, Ltd. (NYC) 1936-41; Pastian Bros. Co. (Rochester, NY) 1932; Philadelphia Badge Co. (Philadelphia, PA) 1931; and others not identified.

P3000 PITCHERS

The earliest pitchers are probably the Japanese made Mickey cream pitchers imported by Borgfeldt. American Pottery, Leeds China Co. and unnamed theme park suppliers have been the major producers of this item.

P3010	Mickey, 4″ or 6″ creamer	10 - 65
P3030	Bambi (American)	5 - 50
P3040	Dumbo Creamer (6″-7″) 3 versions, each	3 - 20
P3045	Dumbo Cream and Sugar (4-1/2″), set	4 - 45
P3046	Dumbo milk pitcher	5 - 35
P3050	Donald Creamer (7″) 3 versions, each	3 - 20
P3070	Snow White or Mickey/Donald, theme park, each	2 - 8

Licensed manufacturers — American Pottery Co. (LA) Bambi set, 1942-48; George Borgfeldt & Co. (NYC) 1930-41; and Leeds China (Chicago) 1944-54.

Also see CHINAWARE and individual ceramic manufacturers.

P3100 PLACEMATS

The record shows a number of placemat licensees, but omits the maker of one of the most common sets, the Wonderful World of Color placemats from 1961, widely distributed by RCA dealers. Despite the wide variety of colorful placemats, collectors have shown little interest. Value 1 - 5 each; Clopaz 2 - 15 each.
Licensed manufacturers — Right of America, Inc. (Summerville, WV) 1982-84; Clopaz Corp. (Cincinnati, OH) 1936-39; Dynamic Merchandising, Inc. (Minn., MN) 1976; Kohn-Goldschmidt, Inc. (NYC) 1941-42; Metro Industries (Philadelphia, PA) 1952-53; Sponge Clean Products (NYC) 1972-73; and The Ullman Co. (Brooklyn, NY) 197?-81.

P3200 PLASTIC TOYS AND NOVELTIES, MISC.

Plastics were used by Disney licensees since the 30's. Use increased after World War II. By 1970, new types of licensees were turning out thousands of different Disney toy items made from plastic. Included were figures, toys, games, playsets, novelties and other items sold from peg board displays, boxes or bins. Toy retailing had changed from the old 5¢ and 10¢ or variety stores to discount toy stores. Whereas licensees of old usually made less than 20 items a year, plastic manufacturers could profitably design and produce a much larger variety of merchandise, often made in Hong Kong or Taiwan. The older plastic toys are beginning to attract collector interest as even the newer items will someday. Manufacturers are provided as a reference for age. Most plastic items are abundantly available at garage sales and flea markets in the 1 - 8 dollar range for the older items.
Licensed manufacturers — Bachmann Brothers, Inc. (Philadelphia, PA) 1935-36, 57-58; Empire of Carolina, Inc., formerly Carolina Enterprises, Inc. (NYC) 1973-84; Famus Corp. (Brooklyn, NY) 1984; Helm Toy Co. (NYC) 1979-84; Illco International Ltd. (NYC) 1983-84; Intoport Development Co. (NYC) 1972-80; Irwin Corp. (Fitchburg, MA) 1949-51; Kohner Bros. (NYC) 1952-56, 68-84; Mego Corp. (NYC) 1977-81; Miner Industries, Inc. and its Multiple Products subsidiary (NYC) 1970-82; Monogram Products, Inc. (Largo, FL) 1972-84; and Precision Specialties, Inc. (LA) 1945-52.

P3400 PLATES — COLLECTOR'S

Miniature collector's plates have been available since the early days of Disneyland. Christmas plates began in 1973 and now different editions are marketed each year by Schmid, Grolier, and Disney theme parks. Grolier followed Schmid's Christmas series in 1979; Disney's own series premiered in 1985. Schmid closed the first Christmas series with 1982 and started over again in 1983. The Grolier plate illustrations are the same as used on each year's bisque figurine, bell and ornament. The Disney series is based on corporate Christmas cards issued 51 years previous. A 500 plate limited edition press giveaway was produced for the premiere of the "A Very Merry Christmas Parade" in 1977. Mother's Day plates began in 1974 and Schmid has produced many other special edition plates. Disney has produced special plates for America on Parade, Mickey's 50th Birthday, Mickey's Greatest Moments, the Disney Classics, Donald's 50th Birthday and other theme park merchandised subjects.

P3420 Disneyland or Walt Disney World miniatures, each 1 - 8
Schmid Collector's Plates (P3450-P3555)

P3450	Christmas '73 "Sleigh Ride"	50 - 200
P3451	Christmas '74 "Decorating the Tree"	40 - 100
P3452	Christmas '75 "Caroling"	5 - 20
P3453	Christmas '76 "Building a Snowman"	6 - 24
P3454	Christmas '77 "Down the Chimney"	5 - 20
P3455	Christmas '78 "Night Before Christmas"	5 - 20
P3456	Christmas '79 "Santa Surprise"	4 - 18
P3457	Christmas '80 "Sleigh Ride"	4 - 18
P3458	Christmas '81 "Happy Holidays"	4 - 18
P3459	Christmas '82 "Winter Games"	4 - 18
P3460	Christmas '83 "Sneak Preview"	4 - 24
P3461	Christmas '84 "Command Performance"	3 - 15
P3500	Mother's Day '74 "Flowers for Mother"	8 - 40
P3501	Mother's Day '75 "Snow White and the 7 Dwarfs"	7 - 30
P3502	Mother's Day '76 "Minnie Mouse and Friends"	6 - 20
P3503	Mother's Day '77 "Pluto's Pals"	5 - 15
P3504	Mother's Day '78 "Flowers for Bambi"	4 - 12
P3505	Mother's Day '79 "Happy Feet"	4 - 12
P3506	Mother's Day '80	4 - 12
P3507	Mother's Day '81	4 - 12

P3100

P3420

P3711

Theme park Bicentennial plates. See America on Parade.

P3503

P3577

P3578

Walt Disney CHARACTERS

Four Seasons of Love Collection
"A Spring Bouquet"
Third Edition in a Series of Four

Walt Disney CHARACTERS

Four Seasons of Love Collection
"Shades of Summer"
Fourth and Final Edition

Walt Disney CHARACTERS

Four Seasons of Love Collection
"Tickets on the 50 Yard Line"
First Edition in a Series of Four

Walt Disney CHARACTERS

Four Seasons of Love Collection
"Let it Snow"
Second Edition in a Series of Four

P3555

P3508	Mother's Day '82	4 - 12
P3524	Bi-Centennial	8 - 40
P3525	Valentine's Day '79 "Hands and Hearts"	6 - 20
P3526	Valentine's Day '80	5 - 15
P3527	Valentine's Day '81	5 - 15
P3530	Zodiac Plates (12), each	4 - 12
P3542	Pinocchio 100th Birthday	4 - 12
P3546	Alice in Wonderland	4 - 12
P3547	Happy Birthday Pluto	4 - 12
P3550	Goofy Golden Jubilee	5 - 15
P3555	Four Seasons of Love Collection (4), each	4 - 12

Grolier Disney Collection merchandise is sold entirely by mail. Limited edition pieces remain available until sold out. Resale on the collector's market is insuffcent to base value ranges at this time. Items produced are listed for collector information only.

P3575	Grolier Christmas '79	
P3576	Grolier Christmas '80	
P3577	Grolier Christmas '81 (Only 6,000 produced vs. 15,000 other years)	
P3578	Grolier Christmas '82	
P3579	Grolier Christmas '83	
P3580	Grolier Christmas '84	
P3581	Grolier Christmas '85	
P3581B	Grolier Christmas '85, bisque	
P3600	Grolier Snow White collection (6)	
P3601	Grolier Pinocchio collection (6)	
P3603	Grolier Bambi collection	
P3604	Grolier Cinderella collection	
P3606	Grolier Peter Pan collection	
P3607	Grolier miniature alphabet series (26)	
P3690	Snow White and the 7 Dwarfs (Goebel) 1980	8 - 45
P3695	Wedgwood Sleeping Beauty Castle (Disneyland) or Cinderella Castle (Walt Disney World), 1st edition, theme park series, each	15 - 50
P3696	2nd edition, Snow White and Dopey in Fantasyland	10 - 35
P3697	3rd edition, Mickey and Minnie on Main Street	10 - 30
P3710	A Very Merry Christmas Parade (limited to 500)	50 - 200
P3711	Mickey's Greatest Moments series (6) Plane Crazy, Steamboat Willie, Brave Little Tailor, Sorcerer's Apprentice, Nifty Fifties (mistake plate), Nifty Nineties, or Mickey Mouse Club, each	4 - 15
P3712	Mickey and Minnie in Concert, bisque	8 - 20
P3713	Disney Classic Series (6) Snow White, Pinocchio, Dumbo, Bambi, Alice in Wonderland or Peter Pan, each	4 - 12
P3720	Disneyland, 25 Years	15 - 40
P3721	Walt Disney World, 10 Years	20 - 40
P3722	Disneyland, 30 Years	20 - 40

WALT DISNEY'S BICENTENNIAL PLATE
1776-1976
LIMITED EDITION

P3524

P3400

P3722

A VERY MERRY CHRISTMAS PARADE
DISNEYLAND 1977

P3710

P3721

P3712

P3730

P3713

P3690

P3460

P3461

P3750

P3800

P3853   P3854   P3855

P3828

P3730 Miniature pewter Mickey film plates, theme park souve-
nirs, each 2 - 6
P3750 Disney Christmas card, '85, sold new for 20
Licensed manufacturers — Goebel (West Germany) 1980-84; Grolier
Enterprises, Inc. (Danbury, CT) 1979-85; Schmid Brothers, Inc. (Boston,
MA) 1970-84; and Wedgwood (England) 1979-84.

P3800 PLAY HOUSES, TENTS, ETC.

O. B. Andrews made 3 sizes of play houses in 1934, the largest
"being big enough for 2 or more children to play inside." The
smaller two were doll house sizes. Crawford Furniture made tents
the same year. Many other manufacturers followed. Most produced such items as part of a broader line such as furniture or play
equipment. The surviving O. B. Andrews paperboard houses are
valued from 50 - 250. Early tents with graphics in good shape
command around 80 - 110. Others from the 40's or later sell for
around 5 - 35 to collectors with a lot of space to store or display
these type items.
Licensed manufacturers — O. B. Andrews (Chattanooga, TN) 1933-35;
Crawford Furniture Mfg. Co. (LA) 1934-35; Come Play Products Co.
(Worcester, MA) 1975-76, corrugated walk-in playhouse; Hettrich Mfg.
Co. (Toledo, OH) 1955, tents; and Natural Science Industries, Ltd. (Far
Rockaway, NY) 1979, vinyl playhouse, toy tunnel and jumpoline.

P3810 PLAYSETS

Playsets combine many small pieces into a themed set designed
to result in hours of imaginary play. Items such as doctor's or
nurses' kits, rocketship control panel, a science laboratory or
entire miniature environments related to Disney characters, films
or other productions. Plastic was the major factor in making
playsets available in the early 50's. Playsets are usually found in
various states of completeness.

P3815	Doctor, nurse, or make-up kits (Hassenfeld) 1951-55, each	5 - 40
P3820	Davy Crockett adventure playset (Gardner)	10 - 60
P3821	Davy Crockett at the Alamo (Marx)	25 - 100
P3825	Walt Disney Television Playhouse (Marx)	40 - 175
P3827	Professer Wonderful's Wonder-Lab (Gilbert)	5 - 35
P3828	Disneyland Rocket Ship Control Board (Baxter)	8 - 40
P3838	Sword in the Stone (Marx)	25 - 100
P3850	Fold-away Disney Playworld (Intoport)	7 - 30
P3851	Doctor or nurse kit (Carolina)	4 - 8
P3853	Robin Hood Adventure (Kusan)	5 - 15
P3854	Mickey Mouse Airlines (Kusan)	5 - 15
P3855	Disneyland Castle (Kusan)	5 - 15

Licensed manufacturers — Azrak-Hamway (NYC) 1975-80, road race
sets; Baxter Co., Inc. (Cincinnati, OH); Concept 2000 aka Intoport Development Co. (NYC) 1972-80; Empire of Carolina, Inc. formerly Carolina
Ent., Inc. (NYC) 1973-84; Gardner & Co. (Chicago) 1955, Davy Crockett
playset; The A.C. Gilbert Co. (New Haven, CN) 1965; Hassenfeld Brothers, Inc. (Pawtucket, RI) 1949-55; and Kusan division of Bethlehem Steel
Corp. (Nashville, TN) 1973-74.

Mickey Mouse
PLAY HOUSES

Made in 3 sizes, the largest size
being big enough for 2 or more
children to play inside. The big
Mickey Mouse Playhouses are the
largest houses ever put on the
market at their price. The Miniature and Tiny Mickey Houses
are exact reproductions of the
larger house.

These fibre board playhouses are
made by the O. B. Andrews
Company, which produces its
own board and does all design-
ing, printing, and cutting in its
own 16 acre plant.

O. B. Andrews Co.
Licensee
Chattanooga, Tenn.
NEW YORK OFFICE
17 East 42nd St.

P3800

P3815

PLAYSET
A three-dimensional panorama of all the scenes and characters from Walt Disney's "The Sword in the Stone," including
Merlin's house, Madam Mim's hut, the castle, knights, drag-
ons, animals and the stars themselves. Packaged in decorative box. $10.98 Suggested retail.

FOR ALL INFORMATION
CONTACT: Louis Marx & Co., Inc.
200 Fifth Avenue
New York, N.Y.

P3838

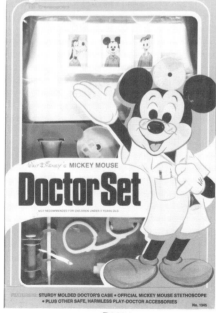

P3851

PROFESSOR WONDERFUL'S WONDER-LAB

DO THE WONDERFUL THINGS THAT PROFESSOR WONDERFUL DOES ON THE MICKEY MOUSE CLUB TV SHOW

FOR AGES 6 TO 12

GILBERT

P3827

WALT DISNEY DISTRIBUTING CO.
P. O. BOX 40, LAKE BUENA VISTA, FLA. 32830 · PH. 824-2222

P4000

GUND MFG. CO.

SITTING ARCHIMEDES OWL (with hat)
WD3491   10½ INCHES
$2 Sug. retail
1 Dozen
Bulk
Pack

SITTING ARCHIMEDES OWL (above)
WD6067   10 INCHES
$3 Suggested retail

HAND PUPPETS

Each has vinyl head, printed cloth body, concealed voice-maker. Height: 11 inches. Three styles: Merlin (illustrated), Wart and Archimedes. Individually packaged in colorful window box.

WD650/2
HAND PUPPET
ASSORTMENT
$1 Suggested retail

STUFFED DOLLS

Plush, cotton stuffed dolls, with vinyl faces, hands, etc., as shown in illustrations. All are in bright, decorative colors. All come in hand-some individual packages, except where bulk packing is indicated.

STANDING ARCHIMEDES OWL (above)
WD7067   14 INCHES
$5 Suggested retail

STANDING MERLIN (not shown)
WD6079   25 INCHES
$8 Suggested Retail

FOR ALL INFORMATION CONTACT:
Gund Manufacturing Co.
200 Fifth Avenue
New York, N.Y.
Attn: Arthur Keller

STANDING MERLIN

MERLIN AS A SQUIRREL

CUDDLE MERLIN THE MAGICIAN

P4000

P4000

WALT DISNEY DISTRIBUTING CO.
P. O. BOX 40, LAKE BUENA VISTA, FLA. 32830 · PH. 824-2222

P4000

22

P4000 PLUSH STUFFED CHARACTERS

It's difficult to draw a distinction between a doll and a plush stuffed character. The latter seems to have developed from the doll in the post war 40's with the advent of synthetic furry materials, plus new fiber and foam stuffing. Thousands of designs have resulted, changing each year as new materials and manufacturing methods are developed. The photos accompanying this section are plush stuffed characters from the 70's merchandise catalogs and Disneyland shop photos from the 80's. Retail stuffed characters range from 5″ to 40″ in height. Value can usually be measured more in love than in dollars, but a representative collection is fun. Licensed manufacturers — California Stuffed Toys division of Cal Fiber Company (LA) 1972-84; Character Novelty Co. (So. Norwalk, CN) 1940-47; Knickerbocker Toy Co., Inc. (Middlesex, NJ) 1976-83; and Plitoys, Inc. (NYC) 1944-45, "washable stuffed toys."

P4000

P4000

P4000

P4000

23

2031 2032 2033 2033

P4000

P5510

P5501

P6005   P6006   P6007   P6035

P5500 POPCORN POPPER & JIFFY POP LIDS

The classic "See 'em Pop" Mickey popcorn popper was made by Empire Products Corp. (Two Rivers, WI) 1935-37. By 1973, popcorn poppers were disposable and American Home Foods (NYC) began promoting magic picture kits "inspired" by Disney films.

P5501	Mickey Mouse popcorn popper (Empire)	35 - 150
P5510	Jiffy Pop popcorn lids (1973-79), each	.50 - 2
P5511	Jiffy Pop magic picture kits, each	.50 - 2

P6000 POSTCARDS

Early Disney postcards were all foreign, produced mainly in England, France or Belgium. The first cards were printed in 1930 by the Inter-Art Co. Cards of similar design were marked "The Milton Post Card" made by Woolstone Bros. of London. G. Delgado of London made postcards c. 1935-36 and the largest producer of early Disney postcards, Valentine & Sons, Ltd., picked up the rights soon thereafter. No Valentine cards show Mickey with pie-cut eyes. All are solid black oval eyes (1935) and later. Valentine cards have postmarks well into the 50's. There were probably between 200-300 different designs. E. Sepheriades, French maker of Superluxe postcards, is noted for their numbered series of cards for *Snow White, Pinocchio, Dumbo* and *Bambi*. An earlier French publisher is not identified. Tobler, a Swiss chocolate maker, packed Walt Disney signed cards in products distributed in France. Several publishers in Belgium were the second largest source of early postcards. Editions Ferraille, W. Hogelbery A. G., and Colorart were publishers of cards posted in Belgium. Edizioni Malano of Italy, plus postcard publishers in Spain, Holland, Germany and many other countries have printed cards. Perhaps Valentine cards were sold in Canada. The earliest American postcards seen have a 1939 postmark. Sun Oil Company began promoting winterizing and other services via postcards in 1940. Walt Disney Productions promoted *The Three Caballeros* with postcards in 1944. The theme parks have been the largest overall source of Disney postcards — well over 2000 different from Disneyland alone. Pre-opening postcards have traditionally been available during the construction process. Collectors are referred to the theme park postcard checklists and historical guides published by R & N Postcard Co., P. O. Box 217, Temple City, CA 91780. There have been oversize, squeaker, and other novelty theme park cards. Also, "card" collection folders to mail or keep as a souvenir, plus bonus books of cards with a photo to keep and a perforated postcard to mail for each scene.

P6005	Inter-Art Mickey cards, each	6 - 20
P6006	Milton postcards, each	6 - 20
P6007	Delgado postcards, each	5 - 18
P6008	Valentine Mickey series, solid oval eyes, each	5 - 15
P6009	Valentine Mickey birthday cards, each	6 - 20
P6010	Valentine Snow White series, 2 versions, each	5 - 18
P6011	Valentine special series such as Ferdinand the Bull, Water Babies and others, each card	5 - 18
P6012	Valentine character cards, white eyes with black pupils, each	5 - 15
P6020	French cartoon character cards, each	4 - 15
P6021	Superlux Snow White series, 24 cards, each	3 - 12
P6022	Superlux Pinocchio series, 24 cards, each	1 - 2
P6023	Superlux Dumbo series, each	2 - 8
P6024	Superlux Bambi series, each	2 - 4
P6030	Tobler chocolate postcards, each	4 - 15
P6035	Other foreign character postcards 30's and 40's	4 - 20
P6036	Same as P6035, except 50's thru present	1 - 5
P6040	Sun Oil promotional postcards, each	4 - 12
P6044	Three Caballeros film promos, each	5 - 29
P6053	Disneyland, pre-opening cards, each	7 - 35
P6055	Disneyland cards with Anaheim, CA directly below logo, each	3 - 12
P6056	Disneyland cards A thru E series, each	1 - 3
P6057	Disneyland, Art Corner, squeaker, character drawings overlaying photo, and other special postcards	1 - 10
P6058	Disneyland black and white photo cards	1 - 12
P6059	Characters in Paris series, sold at park	2 - 20
P6060	Disneyland, postcards of removed attractions	1 - 10
P6061	Hotel or sponsor postcards (such as Monsanto,	

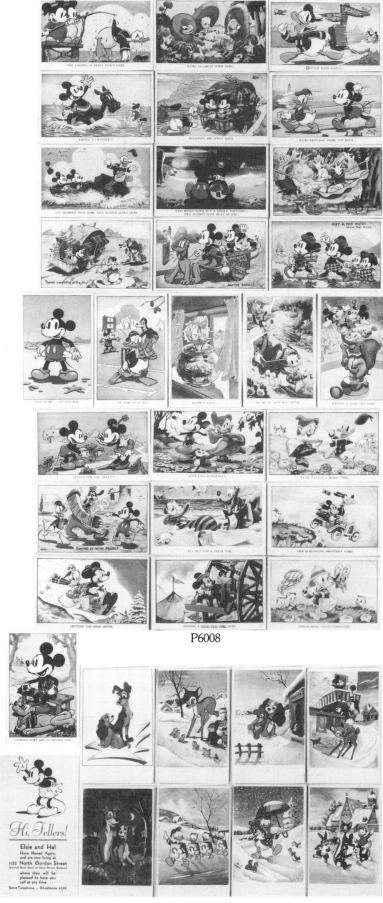

P6008

P6035

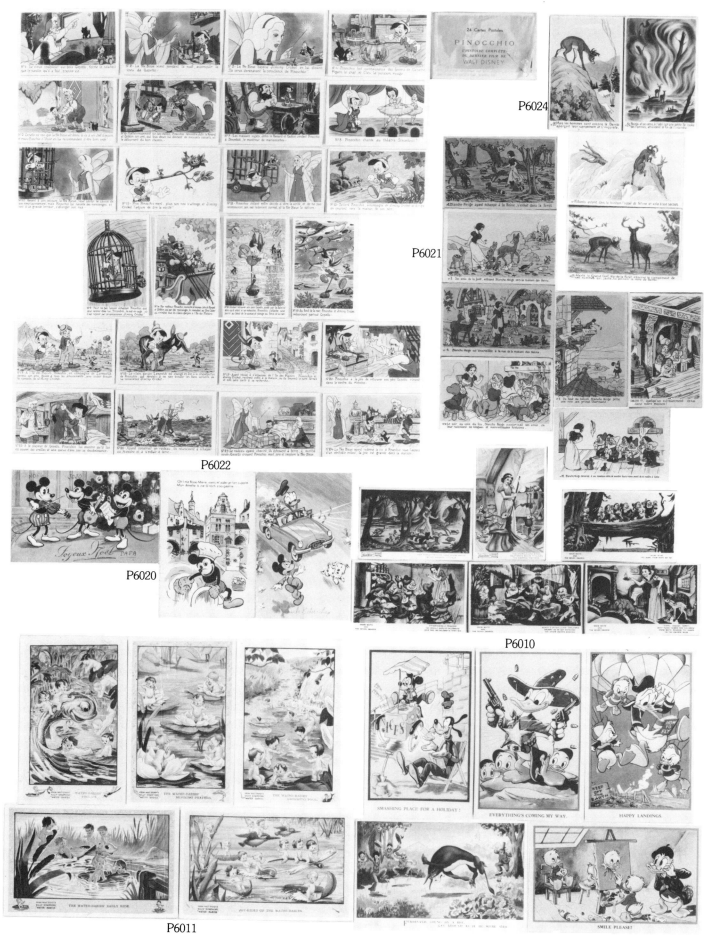

P6024

P6021

P6022

P6020

P6010

P6011

P6012

P6030

P6044

P6009

P6040

P6055

P6057

P6061

P6065

P6053

27

P6057

P6056

P6060

P6066

P6068

P6069

P6066

P6130

28

	Santa Fe, INA, Upjohn, Kaiser or Wurlitzer), each	1 - 2
P6065	Other Disneyland postcards	.25 - 2
P6066	Disneyland bonus books and souvenir folders, each	1 - 5
P6067	Disneyland oversize folders	2 - 15
P6068	Walt Disney World pre-opening without Florida banner	1 - 10
P6069	Walt Disney World Pre-opening with Florida banner	1 - 8
P6070	Walt Disney World cards with Florida banner	1 - 2
P6071	Walt Disney World cards without Florida banner	.25 - 1
P6072	WDW bonus books or folders, each	1 - 5
P6079	EPCOT Center pre-opening, each	1 - 4
P6080	EPCOT Center, each	.25 - 1
P6081	EPCOT Center bonus books or folders, each	1 - 3
P6082	Tokyo Disneyland, pre-opening folder	4 - 15
P6083	Tokyo Disneyland, regular cards, each	1 - 2
P6084	Tokyo Disneyland, New Year cards, each	1 - 5

Licensed U. S. manufacturers and distributors — Angeleno Photo service aka Bob Plunkett (LA) 1956-59; H. S. Crocker (San Bruno, CA) 1955-84; The Dexter Press (NYC) 1967-84; Hallmark Card Co. (Kansas City, KS) 1960-62; Kolorview (LA) 1968; Mitlock & Sons (No. Hollywood, CA) 1954-65; Pictorial Productions (LA) 1957-62; Plastichrome by Colorpicture (Boston) 1954-65; Mike Roberts Color Productions (Berkeley, CA) 1956-67; and Sunoco-Sun Oil Company (Philadelphia, PA) 1938-46.

P6100 POSTERS — CHARACTER

Character posters have been printed by advertisers for premium offers, been licensed for retail sale, and have been used as "gate poster" giveaways at theme parks. Posters are usually printed on a glossy paper rather than a higher quality paper used for art prints.

P6110	Advertiser premiums	2 - 15
P6130	Character posters sold at Disney theme parks, newsstands, and other retailers	2 - 10
P6160	Theme park gate posters	2 - 12

Licensed manufacturers — American Publishing Corp. (Watertown, MA) 1979-84; Pro-Arts (Medina, OH) 1979; and Renselaar Corp. (Conshohocken, PA) 1970-71.

P6200 POSTERS — MOVIE

Movie poster collecting is a specialized area of Disneyana. Many collectors are oriented more toward films than toys or memorobilia. Posters were generic at first, but most animated shorts and all features had special posters. Features often had 2 or 3 different posters with each release until the 50's. Each feature film re-release has traditionally had new graphic treatments on all advertising materials, including posters in 2 or 3 sizes. As production of new animated short cartoons ground to a halt in the early 50's, generic posters were revived by RKO. Movie posters for animated feature films since 1955 sell for 10 - 40 each depending on the film. Live action film posters are valued at 1 - 10. The first generic Mickey Mouse posters (1928-30) bring several hundred dollars. Cartoon short posters from the 30's 40's and 50's start at around 100 and are often priced from 300 to 1000. They sell well in the 100 - 300 range. Original release pre-war animated feature posters are the most valuable and are sometime priced above 500. The other animated feature posters from 1945-52 can command 65 - 200 or more in Hollywood. Serigraph 8-color silkscreen reproductions of Disney cartoon short posters are produced by Circle Fine Art Corp. (Chicago) for sale at art galleries and theme park Disneyana shops for 20 each. Springbok division of Hallmark Cards, Inc. reproduced the Two-Gun Mickey poster around 1975, valued at 1 - 4.

P6500 POSTERS — OTHER

Disney employee recruitment posters distributed to art schools, travel posters and art exhibit posters are examples of other type posters. The Disney Studio did a number of war effort posters (see WORLD WAR II) and numerous advertising posters for various licensees (see ADVERTISING SIGNS). The Disney films and characters have been the theme of stage shows, parades, public service campaigns on dental health, literacy, prevention of forest fires, safety and other subjects.

| P6505 | Disney Studio artist recruitment, each | 5 - 50 |
| P6525 | Theme park and other travel posters, each | 1 - 10 |

P6130

P6200

29

P6825

P6865

P6825

P6800

P6829

P7100

P6825

P6550	Art exhibit posters, each	1 - 15
P6575	Other posters, 30's, each	5 - 50
P6576	Other posters, 40's, each	4 - 40
P6577	Other posters, 50's to present, depending on age, subject and collectibility	1 - 25

P6800 POTTIES

Porcelain-clad metal potties were imported by Borgfeldt and Krueger in the early 30's. Walt Disney's personal gift to friends with a new baby was a ceramic potty with characters in relief. Each was personalized with the new arrival's name. Even though they were ordered in quantities of 500, few owners are known to have parted with such a special gift. The author will pay $200 for an undamaged one.

P6805	Potty, porcelain clad	50 - 200
P6810	Walt Disney gift potties	?

P6825 PREMIUMS — MISCELLANEOUS

Kay Kamen understood the tremendous value of free giveaways. One of his first promotions was to give away Mickey Mouse dollars good for a free ice cream cone. He created buttons, balloons and special Christmas premiums. He encouraged each licensee to do the same, and the widespread use of Disneyana premiums took on many forms. Only premiums not appropriate to other classifications are listed here. The list will undoubtably grow in future years.

P6825	Play money or movie circles from comic strips, each	.25 - 2
P6829	Album of My Favorite Picture Stars, theater giveaway	4 - 12
P6830	Mickey Mouse or Snow White photos for P6829, each	5 - 25
P6865	Mickey Mouse Club magic kit (Mars)	5 - 20

Licensed manufacturers — Kay Kamen Ltd. (NYC) 1936-41 and Cramer-Tobias-Meyer, Inc. (NYC) 1939-41, printed promotional specialties.

P7100 PRESS BOOKS — FILM

A press book is distributed to theater operators for information on film background, publicity materials, promotional tie-ins and advertising. Each press book is printed. There are no glossy photos. Often there is a merchandise or ad pad supplement. Its basic function is to provide needed material for advertising and limited print publicity. The rest is drum beating to get operators to run larger size ads. Even some of the old cartoons had four page press books. These bring 35 - 100 each. Original pre-1955 animated feature press books are the most sought after, bringing 35 -200 for exceptional examples. The 1955 *Lady and the Tramp* and pressbooks thereafter include merchandise licensees that are of double interest to collectors. These are valued from 8 - 50 each, depending on age, original release, merchandise content and

P6505

P6550

P7100

P7100

P7100

P7259

P7256

P7261

P7260

completeness. Press books for animated films released after the original release of *101 Dalmatians* are in greater supply and sell in the 4 - 18 range. Live action film press books rarely sell for over 8.

P7250 PRINTING SETS

Fulton Specialty and Marks Bros. produced the first rubber stamp printing sets in 1933-34. Fulton continued till 1942 and produced many highly collectible sets. The George Borgfeldt Corp. was licensed for printing sets exclusively for 1949-50. Multi-Print of Milan, Italy made an exceptional series of printing sets on a foreign license in the 70's. These were imported and sold by major department stores and Disney theme parks.

P7251	Oswald the Lucky Rabbit stencil set	75 - 200
P7255	Mickey Mouse Printing and Coloring Set (Marks Bros.)	25 - 100
P7256	Mickey Mouse Print Shop (Fulton) 3 sizes	10 - 50
P7257	Mickey Mouse Picture Printing Set (Fulton) 3 sizes	10 - 50
P7258	Bad Wolf/3 Pig Artistamp Picture Set (Fulton) 2 sizes	15 - 75
P7259	Donald Duck Art Stamp Picture Set (Fulton) 3 sizes	15 - 75
P7260	Snow White and 7 Dwarfs Art Stamp Picture Set (Fulton) 2 sizes	10 - 65
P7261	Pinocchio Art Stamp Picture Set (Fulton) 2 sizes	15 - 75
P7275	Sword in the Stone printer set (Colorforms)	5 - 15
P7280	Italian Multi-Print sets, 2 sizes, Snow White, Winnie the Pooh, Dumbo, Jungle Book and Carousel (main characters), each	5 - 25
P7285	Mickey's Printing Set (Straco)	1 - 3

Licensed manufacturers — H. Barnard Stamp & Stencil Co., Ltd. (perhaps a supplier of printing sets distributed by Borgfeldt) 1949-50; George Borgfeldt Corp. (NYC) 1949-50; Colorforms (Norwood, NJ) 1963-64; Fulton Specialty Co. (NYC) 1933-42; International Games, Inc. (Joliet, IL) 1981-83; Multi-Print (Milan, Italy) c. 1975-80, importer unknown; and Straco F. J. Strauss, Co., Inc. (No. Bergen, NJ) 1976-84.

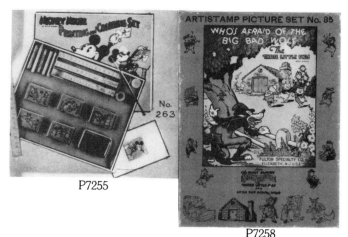

P7255

P7258

FULTON FAULTLESS EDUCATIONAL TOY

P7256

P7275

P7257

33

P7280

P7285

P7310

P7311

P7312

P7313

P7315

P7316

P7317

P7314

34

P7300 PRINTS — ART AND FRAMED PICTURES

The first framed pictures, Reliance by Bates Art Industries, were reproduced "cel like" on the back of glass. Courvoisier Galleries released the first art prints in 1940. Henry A. Citroen sold an extensive line of luminous pictures in white frames from 1944-46. The New York Graphic Society followed with prints from Snow White and Bambi in 1947. Disney marketing department artist Charles Boyer did a Walt Disney take-off painting of Norman Rockwell's "Self Portrait" for the cover of an employee magazine in 1978. Many recipients requested framable copies, and Boyer did a signed/numbered edition of 1,800. These were sold to employees for $4 each. Its success led to many other Boyer limited edition lithographs. Another Rainbow has produced a series of Carl Barks signed lithographs. Disney artist John Hench signed a 750 limited edition of the 25th and 50th Mickey Mouse birthday paintings he created. An employee drawing was held for the right to purchase a portfolio of the two prints for $50 each in 1978.

P7305   Reliance glass pictures, 3 Pigs, Red Riding Hood and Big Bad Wolf (8 different) or Mickey, Minnie, Horace and Clarabelle (? different), Bates Art Industries, each   15 - 150

Courvorsier Galleries P7310-17 (came framed or in mailing envelope)

P7310	Pinocchio with Jiminy Cricket on foot	15 - 50
P7311	Geppetto creating Pinocchio	15 - 50
P7312	Pinocchio, Jiminy Cricket, Figaro and Cleo	15 - 50
P7313	Pinocchio, Geppetto and Figaro on raft	15 - 50
P7314	Mickey and Pluto	20 - 60
P7315	Donald and Better Self	20 - 60
P7316	Bunnies in bed	10 - 40
P7317	Snow White with Forest Animals	15 - 50
P7320	Citroen luminous pictures — Mickey, Minnie,	

LITHOGRAPHED PRINTS

Full-color lithographed prints of Bambi and His Forest Friends and others. Practical for children's rooms, Walt Disney Character prints can be ordered with special freplex frames. These frames eliminate glass, using in its place a durable shellac topcoat that's easily cleaned with a damp cloth.

"Bambi Meets His Forest Friends" (print only) . . . 26934 (20" x 24") . . . $4 retail. 25934 (15" x 18") . . . $2 retail; 25934 (10" x 12") . . . $1 retail
"Snow White's Last Call For Dinner" (print only) . . . 26935 (20" x 24") . . . $4 retail. 25935 (15" x 18") . . . $2 retail; 25935 (10" x 12") . . . $1 retail
"Forest Secrets, Told by Thumper To Bambi" (print only) . . . 26936 (20" x 24") . . . $4 retail; 25936 (15" x 18") . . . $2 retail; 25936 (10" x 12") . . . $1 retail
"Good Friends, All!" (print only) . . . 26937 (20" x 24") . . . $4 retail; 25937 (20" x 24") . . . $2 retail; 25937 (10" x 12") . . . $1 retail
Framing Prices According To Specifications

NEW YORK GRAPHIC SOCIETY
10 WEST 33rd STREET, NEW YORK, 1, N. Y.
Chicago, Ill.—Merchandise Mart • Los Angeles, Calif.—10465 Troon Ave.

57

P7324

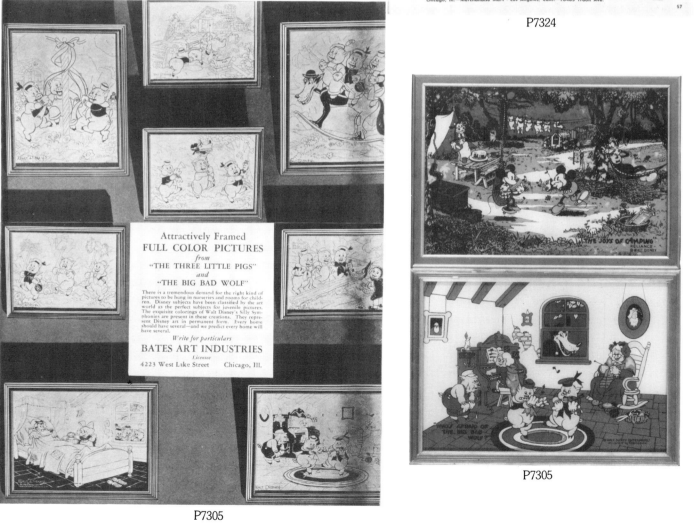

Attractively Framed
FULL COLOR PICTURES
from
"THE THREE LITTLE PIGS"
and
"THE BIG BAD WOLF"

There is a tremendous demand for the right kind of pictures to be hung in nurseries and rooms for children. Disney subjects have been classified by the art world as the perfect subjects for juvenile pictures. The exquisite colorings of Walt Disney's Silly Symphonies are present in these creations. They represent Disney art in permanent form. Every home should have several—and we predict every home will have several.

Write for particulars

BATES ART INDUSTRIES
Licensee
4223 West Lake Street   Chicago, Ill.

P7305

P7305

P7425

P7324

P7324

P7320

36

Donald, Goofy, Donald and Mickey, Bambi,
Thumper, Thumper and girlfriend, Snow White
and forest animals, Wynken, Blynken and Nod
and others, each   2 - 12

P7324   New York Graphic Society, Snow White (2 different) or
         Bambi (2 different), each   10 - 25
         "Self Portrait" (Boyer) see F2105

P7350	"Partners" (Boyer)	75 - 300
P7351	"The Band" (Boyer)	40 - 100
P7352	"New Fantasyland" (Boyer)	35 - 75
P7353	"Tokyo Disneyland" (Boyer)	30 - 70
P7354	"Disneyland 30th Year" (Boyer)	5 - 30

         John Hench Mickey 50th Birthday portfolio (see F2110)

Licensed manufacturers — Artisto, Inc. (NYC) 1938-39, framed pictures;
Bates Art Industries (Chicago) 1934-35; Henry A. Citroen (NYC) 1944-46;
Courvoisier Galleries (San Francisco and NYC) 1938-46, also sold cels;
Econolite Corp. (LA) 1955-58, silkscreen pictures; E.P.I.C., Inc. (Philadel-
phia, PA) 1968; Hales Pictures, Inc. (NYC) 1937-38, poster pictures; New
York Graphic Society (NYC) 1945-49, 68-70; Picture That, Inc. (Mel-
bourne, FL) 1980-84; Reliance Picture Frame Co. (see Bates Art Indus-
tries); and The Trimart Co. (NYC) 1945-46, framed felt pictures.

         Also see — WALL DECORATIONS

P7400 PROGRAMS — MOVIE, SPECIAL SHOWS AND EVENTS

     There are movie programs of several types: premiere, souvenir,
benefit showings and theater giveaways. Special shows and events
include parades, shows, public appearances, even performances
to raise financing.

P7425	Radio City Music Hall Snow White program	5 - 35
P7430	Fantasia souvenir program	8 - 30
P7437	Song of the South souvenir program	6 - 24
P7445	Sleeping Beauty premiere program	8 - 25
P7447	Mary Poppins souvenir program	2 - 12
P7450	The Happiest Millionaire sourvenir program	2 - 10
P7457	Black Hole premiere programs	1 - 5
P7458	Fox and Hound premiere programs	1 - 10
P7465	Silver Screen Partners II	1 - 2

         Also see — DISNEYLAND, EPCOT CENTER, ICE SHOWS,
TOKYO DISNEYLAND and WALT DISNEY WORLD.

P7500 PROJECTION EQUIPMENT

     The Movie Jecktors and Keystone 16mm movie projectors of
the 30's plus the picture guns and the Mickey Mouse Club type
projectors of the 50's are the major collectibles in this classification. The Movie Jecktors are particularly unique and fascinating.
The paper film strips have parallel comic strips with slight variations in words and character positions. When the Movie Jecktor is
operated, a shutter alternates between the two separate projec-
tion lenses focused on each strip, creating a limited animation
effect as the strip slowly passes through the machine frame by
frame. Picture guns were popular in the 50's.
         Mickey Mouse Toy Lantern Outfit (see L2000)

P7505	Movie Jecktor	25 - 95
P7506	Movie Jecktor paper filmstrips, each	3 - 15
P7507	Talkie Jecktor	50 - 125
P7508	Talkie Jecktor picture records, each	35 - 175
P7509	Talkie Jecktor records, regular, each	5 - 15
P7512	Mickey Mouse movie projector (Keystone) 1935	45 - 150
P7513	Mickey Mouse movie projector (Keystone) 1936	25 - 100
P7525	Mickey Mouse Club or Donald Duck projectors (Stephens)	5 - 20
P7527	Mickey Mouse Club Auto-magic picture gun (Stephens)	5 - 30
P7528	Davy Crockett Auto-magic picture gun (Stephens)	5 - 28

Licensed manufacturers — Collund Mfg. Corp. (LA) 1947, toy motion
picture projects; Keystone Mfg. Co. (Boston) 1935-37; Mastercraft Toy
Co., Inc. (NYC) 1946-48, toy projector (zoetrope); Movie Jecktor Co., Inc.
(NYC) 1935-37; Stephens Products Co., Inc. later Philson Industries now
Worchester Toy Products Co. (Middletown, CT) 1953-57; and Transo-
gram Co., Inc. (NYC) 1968-71, 8mm movie projector.
         Also see — FILMS, SLIDES AND VIEWERS

P7600 PUBLICITY KITS

     Publicity kits are an extension of press books in film promotion.
They include glossy still photographs and press releases designed

P7430

P7445

P7512

P7505   P7506

P7508

P7525

P7527

P7528

P7507   P7509

P7513

P7600

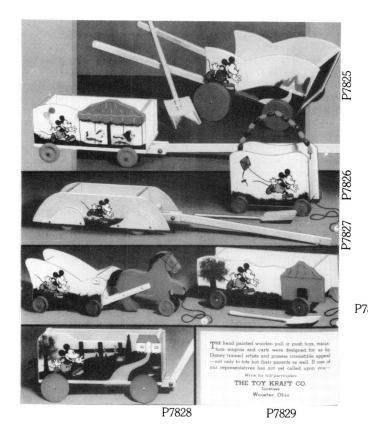

P7825

P7826

P7827

P7828   P7829

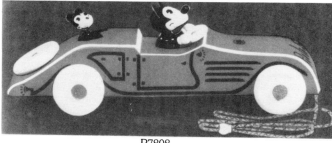

P7808

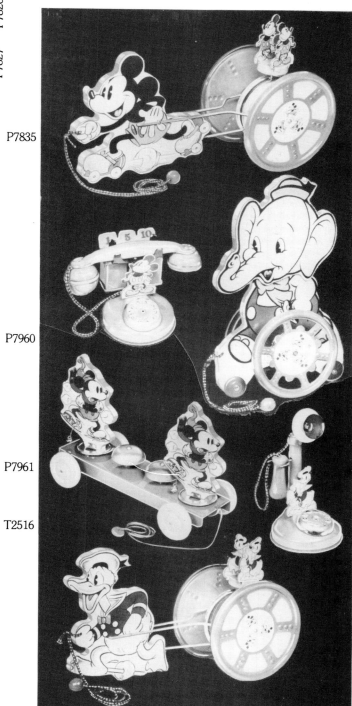

P7835

P7960

P7961

T2516

P7962

P7823   P7822   P7820   P7816   P7821

T2512   P7817

P7837

P7839

P7966

T2525   P7967

P7963

T2526

P7964   P7965

P7970

P7971   T2530   P7972

to make a reporter's job easier and obtain more "free" print publicity. Disney television and theme parks also make extensive use of publicity kits. Older kits are particularly valuable if complete (very rare). They must be individually judged for value. Modern kits used for re-release, however, re-use much of the same material. A variety of kits since 1960 can be purchased for 10 - 25 each.

P7800 PULL TOYS

Many manufacturers made push or pull toys as part of their line. Several specialized. The leading producers of classic Disney pull toys were Fisher-Price (see F7600) and the N. N. Hill Brass Company. Other manufacturers are noted with item.

P7840

P7842

P7943

P7808	Mickey wood car (Borgfeldt)	50 - 150
P7815	Pluto pulling twin revolving Mickeys (1934)	25 - 125
P7816	Revolving Mickeys, 4 wheels (1934)	20 - 100
P7817	Mickey, 2 wheels, with handle (1934)	15 - 65
P7820	Tanglefoot pulling large fixed Mickey (1935)	20 - 100
P7821	Tanglefoot pulling small revolving Mickey (1935)	15 - 75
P7822	Horace pulling 2 bell wheels (1935)	15 - 75
P7823	Long bill Donald pulling 2 bell wheels (1935)	25 - 95
P7825	Mickey wheelbarrow (Toy Kraft) 1935	15 - 55
P7826	Mickey kite pull cart with handle (1935)	15 - 50
P7827	Running Mickey wagon (Toy Kraft) 1935	15 - 55
P7828	Mickey horse cart (Toy Kraft) 1935	15 - 60
P7829	Mickey house or tent wagon (Toy Kraft) 1935	15 - 55
P7835	Mickey or Donald 2 wheel with revolving Mickeys (1936)	15 - 75
P7837	Horace or Pluto pulling small Mickey, 2 wheel (1936)	15 - 55
P7839	Medium bill Donald, 2 bell wheels (1936)	15 - 50
P7840	Mickey's head or full figure hobby-horses (1936)	25 - 100
P7842	Mickey on belly, 4 wheel pull toy (1936)	20 - 80
P7943	Bank pull toy	20 - 80
P7944	Large Mickey on two bell wheels	20 - 70
P7950	Toy Kraft Mickey or Donald 2 horse cart (1936)	15 - 50
P7952	Wagon, Mickey with Pluto or with elephant (1936)	15 - 55
P7960	Large Elmer Elephant, 2 wheel (1938)	20 - 65
P7961	2 ice skating Mickeys on bell cart (1938)	25 - 100
P7962	Donald pulling 2 revolving Donalds, 2 wheel (1938)	20 - 75
P7963	Snow White and Prince on bell cart (1938)	20 - 75
P7964	Seven Dwarfs pulling Snow White (1938)	20 - 75
P7965	Dopey and Doc pulling Snow White (1938)	20 - 75
P7966	Seven Dwarfs pulling 2 wheel bell ringer (1938)	15 - 50
P7967	Dopey and Doc pulling cart with small Snow White and Dopey atop two wheel bell ringer (1938)	15 - 65
P7970	Ferdinand and Matador bell cart (1940)	20 - 65
P7971	Pinocchio and Figaro (1940)	18 - 60
P7972	Pinocchio and Cleo (1940)	18 - 65
P7985	Lady and the Tramp pull toy (Eldon) 1955	12 - 35
P7986	Strombeck-Becker wooden pull toys, each	10 - 25

Licensed manufacturers — Geo. Borgfeldt & Co. (NYC) 1931-41; Cragston Corp. (NYC) 1968-71; Eldon Mfg. Co. (LA) 195; Fisher-Price (see F7600); The N. N. Hill Brass Co. (East Hampton, CN) 1933-42; Strombeck-Becker Mfg. Co. (Moline, IL) 1955-59; and Toy Kraft Co. (Wooster, OH) 1933-37.

P8000 PUPPETS AND MARIONETTES

There have been Mickey and Minnie marionettes since 1930 when Bullock's Wilshire department store had them produced. Borgfeldt offered a Steiff hand puppet in 1932. Madame Alexander, Gund Manufacturing, and Peter Puppet Playthings have been the largest U. S. makers. Pelham Puppets Ltd. of Marlborough, England is not a U. S. licensee, but their puppets have been regularly imported since the 50's at least.

P7944   T2513

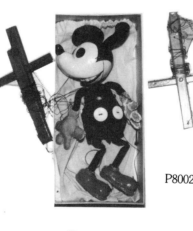

P8002

P8002	Mickey or Minnie marionette	150 - 500
P8005	Mickey Steiff hand puppet	65 - 400
P8010	Alexander marionettes, Mickey or Minnie	50 - 150
P8012	Pluto or Donald (Alexander)	35 - 120
P8014	Snow White or Wicked Queen (Alexander)	60 - 120
P8016	Prince, Huntsman or Hag (Alexander)	50 - 80
P8019	Seven Dwarfs (Alexander), each	30 - 70
P8025	Tumbling Mickey — pie eyes (Marks Bros.)	10 - 30
P8026	Tumbling Mickey — 1947 (Marks Bros.)	12 - 35
P8030	Donald or Pluto string puppet (Modern	

P8005

P8010   P8019   P8012

P8030

P8016   P8014

PLAY WITH
Walt Disney's
PLUTO
"STRING"
PUPPET

P8040

42

	Record Albums), each	12 - 35
P8035	Dopey, composition head hand puppet (Canadian)	8 - 32
P8040	Mickey, Minnie, Donald or Pluto hand puppets (Gund) 1949, each	2 - 12

By 1960 Gund produced 25 or so different character hand puppets. The heads are all rubber with cloth mitt-like bodies. Earlier versions used bright colored cloth with no attempt at making it look like the character's costume. Later versions had the character's body printed on white cloth.

P8044	Additional Gund Disney character hand puppets include Dopey, Peter Pan, Tinker Bell, Capt. Hook, Wendy, Lady, Tramp, Dachsie, Pedro, Sleeping Beauty Princess, King Stefan, Flora, Fauna, Merryweather, Horace Horsecollar, Geppetto, and a Babes in Toyland series (1961), each	2 - 10
P8075	Peter Puppet marionettes, main characters, plus Lady and the Tramp, company used vinyl heads, painted composition bodies, and often sponge rubber feet, each	5 - 25
P8090	Pinocchio/Jiminy Cricket Campbell's premium	4 - 20
P8100	Pelham marionettes	5 - 35

Licensed manufacturers — Alexander Doll Co. (NYC) 1933-39, 51-53, 59; George Borgfeldt & Co. (NYC) 1930-50; Bullock's Wilshire (LA) 1930; Durham Industries, Inc. (NYC) 1972-83, pocket puppets; Gund Mfg. Co. (NYC) 1947-71; Kohner Bros., Inc. (East Patterson, NJ) 1972-84, trapeze toys, push button puppets, string and mini puppets; Modern Record Albums, Toy division (College Point, NY) 1949-50; Peter Puppet Playthings, Inc. (Long Island City, NY) 1951-58; Questor Education Products (Bronx, NY) 1972-77, finger puppets; Rubber for Molds, Inc. (Chicago) 1948-49, hand puppets; and Whitman Publishing Co. (Racine, WI) 1934-85, paperboard "storytime puppets".

P8090

P8044

P8025

P8026

McCall pattern puppet. Value 1-8.

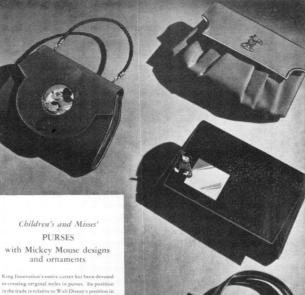

P8500

P8500

P8500 PURSES AND HANDBAGS

Herz & Kory made "children's pocketbooks in 1931. Cohn & Rosenberger (see Jewelry at J2050-J2056) produced a delightful series of mesh and enameled metal coin purses beginning in 1932. A steady stream of licensees have followed. Most cloth purses have tattered with use and have been discarded. Excellent examples of early 30's purses and bags may command up to 50. Average condition pieces from the same period and those of any subsequent year might bring 1 - 25.

Licensed manufacturers — Centra Leather Goods Corp. (NYC) 1948-49; Debway Corp. (NYC) 1952-53; Elliot Knitwear Corp. (1950) later Elliot International, Inc. (NYC) 1972-83; The Herrmann Handkerchief Co., Inc. (NYC) 1932-51 (see HANDKERCHIEFS); Herz & Kory (NYC) 1931-33; King Innovations, Inc. (NYC) 1934-36; Lanco Handbag Co., Inc. (NYC) 1984, purses and coin purses; Lorraine Novelty Mfg. Co., Inc. (NYC) 1933-34; Pyramid Leather Goods Inc. (NYC) 1938-43; Salient, Inc. (E. Longmeadow, MA) 1951-52 1 M. Slifka & Sons (NYC) 1932, 47-57; and Troy Sunshade Co. (Troy, OH) 1935, carrier bags and aprons.

P9000 PUZZLES AND PUZZLE SETS

Saalfield Publishing and Marks Brothers Company supplied puzzles in the early 30's. Whitman began producing puzzle sets around 1938. Jaymar Specialty Company began with jigsaw puzzles in 1943 and eventually produced other types as well. Other types of puzzles include: tray (have solid border and cardboard back — puzzle is sold and stored put together), wood, magnetic, premium, or puzzle games (see GAMES — PUZZLE)

P9205	Mickey Mouse Hosiery "T" puzzle	5 - 30
P9206	Marks Brothers picture puzzles, each	10 - 50
P9207	Marks Brothers hand puzzles, each	10 - 50
P9210	Saalfield picture puzzle set (4)	35 - 125
P9215	Snow White and 7 Dwarfs set (2) Whitman	10 - 40
P9516	Different puzzles used in P9215, each	2 - 10
P9550	First series Jaymar jigsaw puzzles, paper wrapped boxes, Mickey Mouse, Snow White & 7 Dwarfs, 3 Pigs and 1 other. Illustration surrounding puzzle on sign board is a rural setting featuring Donald, Mickey, Goofy, Snow White, Dopey, Bashful and forest animals (1943), each of 4 puzzles	4 -15

P9207

P9205

P9206

P9210

P9215

P9516

P9550

P9554

P9558

P9580

P9580

P9585

P9568

P9600

P9710

P9610

P9660

P9620

46

P9554 Same as P9550, except printed direct on paper-
       board box (c. 1944), each   3 - 12
P9558 Second series, Mickey and Donald working jigsaw
       puzzle on box cover, complete picture in lower
       right corner, scenes include Bambi, Dumbo,
       Gremlins, Saludos Amigos, and main character
       scenes (c. 1944-46)   4 - 16
P9568 Same puzzles as P9550, but puzzles are inter-
       locking, boxes have blue trim with white dots.
       Donald and Nephews playing hockey is fourth
       puzzle in this series (1947), each   3 - 12
P9580 Boxed set for four tray puzzles (Jaymar)
       Mickey, Donald, Pluto and 3 Pigs (1947)   10 - 50
P9580 Same puzzles, unboxed, each   2 - 8
P9585 Whitman, four different boxed sets of two picture
       puzzles, one box each for Mickey, Goofy, Pluto
       and Donald (1949), each box   8 - 22
P9600 Series of 8 Jaymar jigsaw puzzles (1949)
       Mickey, Donald, Snow White, 3 Pigs, Grasshopper
       and the Ants, The Ugly Duckling, Tortoise and
       the Hare, and Pinocchio, each   3 - 16
P9610 Cinderella jigsaw or tray puzzles, each   3 - 12
P9620 Alice in Wonderland jigsaw or tray puzzles, each 3 - 14

P9755

P9640

P9730

P9780

47

P9790

P9791

P9760

P9740

P9792

P9820

48

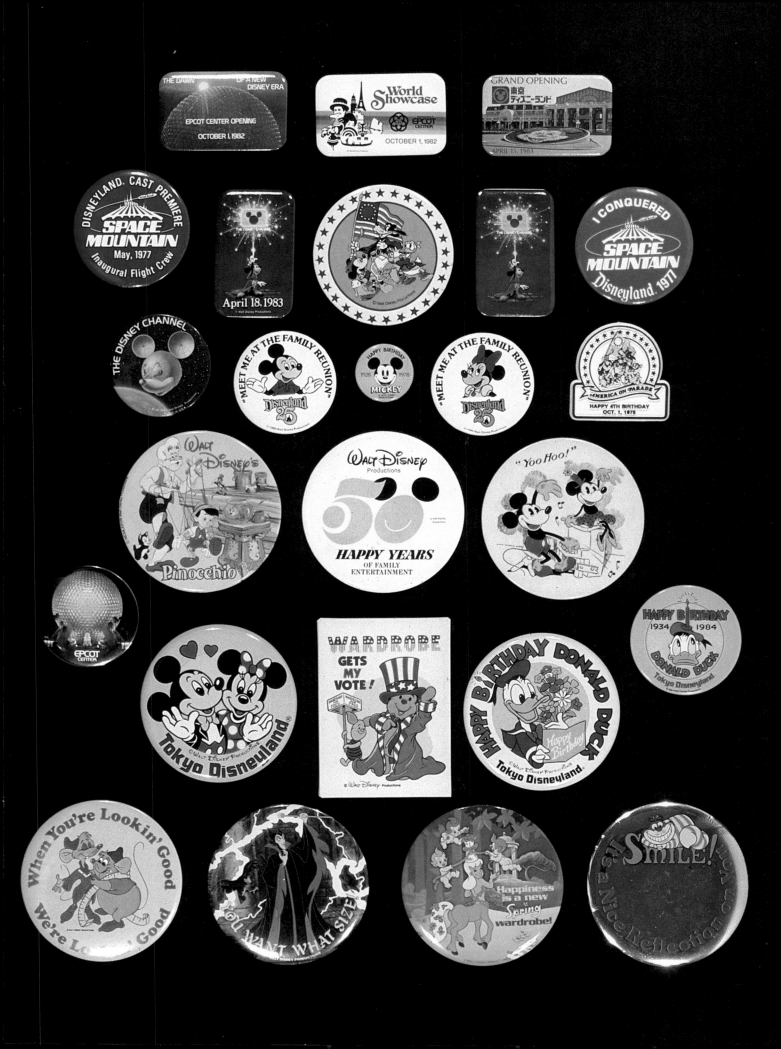

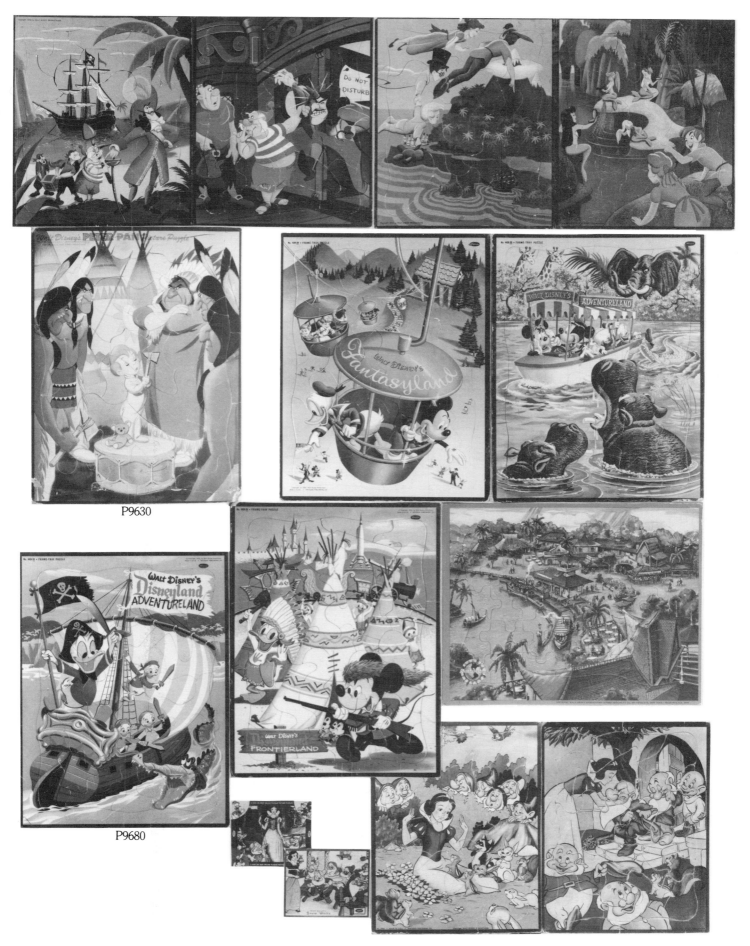

P9630

P9680

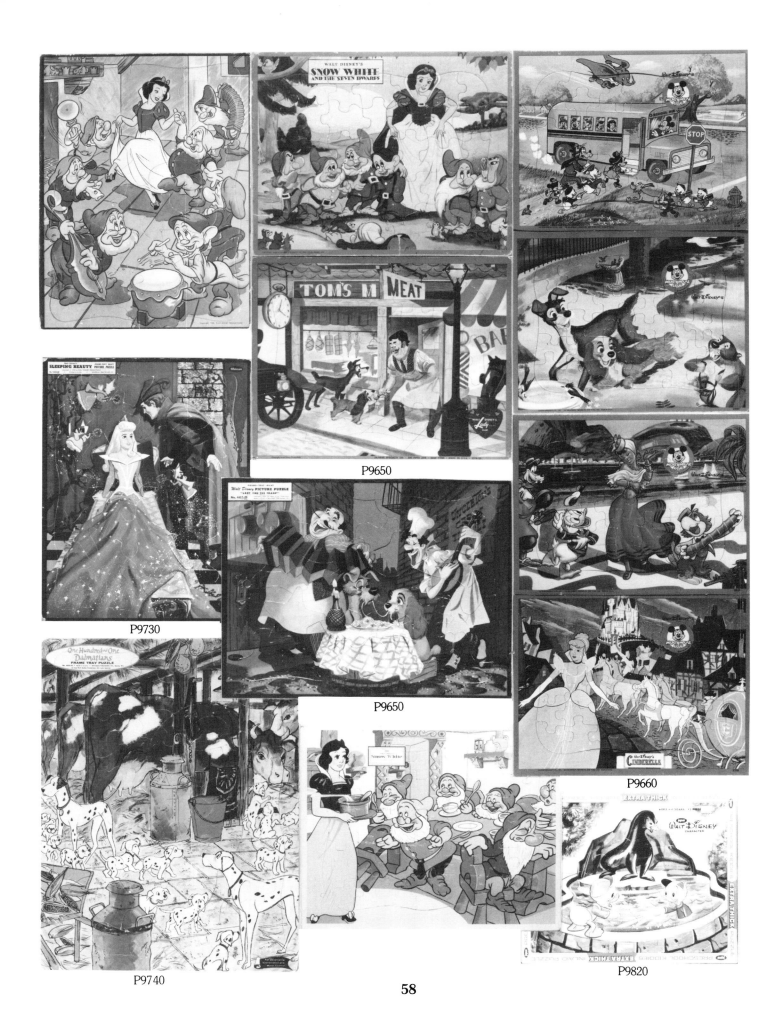

P9650

P9730

P9650

P9660

P9740

P9820

58

P9630	Peter Pan jigsaw or tray puzzles, each		3 - 14
P9640	Main character jigsaw puzzles, series 2050, (4)		
	Toyland, Auto Ride, Wash Day or Hayloft, each		3 - 14
P9650	Lady and the Tramp, jigsaw or tray, each		3 - 12
P9660	Mickey Mouse Club, jigsaw or tray' each		3 - 12
P9680	Disneyland, jigsaw or tray puzzles, each		3 - 12
P9710	Davy Crockett or Zorro, jigsaw or tray, each		3 - 12
P9730	Sleeping Beauty, jigsaw or tray, each		3 - 12
P9740	Other jigsaw or tray puzzles from 50's, each		3 - 12
P9755	Wood, magnetic or other type puzzles 40's or 50's, each		5 - 20
P9760	Jigsaw or tray puzzles, 60's, each		3 - 10
P9780	Other types of puzzles, 50's or 60's, each		4 - 16
P9790	Jigsaw or tray puzzles, 70's, each		2 - 8
P9791	Collector's puzzles, 70's or 80's, each		3 - 10
P9792	Other type puzzles, 70's or 80's, each		3 - 10
P9820	Jigsaw or tray puzzles, 80's, each		1 - 5

Notice — Many puzzles have been reissued. The pictures shown do not conclusively date the puzzle in all cases.

Licensed manufacturers — Child Guidance Toys, Inc. (Bronx, NY) 1964-71, magnetic puzzles; Jaymar Specialty Co. (NYC) 1943-84; The Judy Company (Minneapolis, MN) 1944-50; Marks Brothers Company (Boston) 1934-41, 46-48; Parker Brothers (NYC) 1933-41, 47-84, puzzle games; Questor Education Products division of Questor Corp. (Bronx, NY) 1972-77, magnetic puzzles; Saalfield Publishing Co. (Akron, OH) 1931-37; and Whitman Publishing Co. (Racine, WI) 1933-85.

P9780

P9780

P9790

59

P9780

P9800

P9820

R1000

R1045

R1028

R1055

R1000

R1000 RADIOS, PHONOGRAPHS AND TAPE PLAYERS

Emerson radios and phonographs were produced from 1933-40. RCA made an Alice in Wonderland 45 rpm player in 1951. GE clock radios give the initial appearance of being made in the 50's, but records indicate they were produced in 1970-71. There may be other collectible radios or phonographs. Noblitt-Sparks is recorded as a late 30's maker, however, the author hasn't run across one yet. This company may also have been making the Emerson products. Radios since the 60's are much smaller and have been produced largely of plastic in Japan and Taiwan. A reproduction of the Emerson Mickey "carved" radio was made in the 1970's.

R1005	Mickey, brown "carved" radio (1933-39)	250 - 750
R1006	Mickey, white or black radio with aluminum plate over grill cloth	200 - 700
R1008	Mickey phonograph (Emerson)	150 - 800
R1010	Snow White radio	150 - 600
R1025	Alice in Wonderland phonograph (RCA)	25 - 75
R1028	Donald Duck electric phonograph (Spears)	10 - 45
R1040	Show 'n Tell phonograph/viewers (GE)	5 - 20
R1045	Mickey, Donald or Pooh phonographs	5 - 20
R1055	Character transistor radios, each	4 - 15

Licensed manufacturers — Childstar, Ltd. (NYC) 1974-84, silver and woodgrain table radios; Emerson Radio & Phonograph Corp. (NYC) 1933-40; General Electric Co. (Utica, NY) 1970-71; Hudson Electronics Corp. (Mt. Vernon, NY) 1953, phonographs; Interstate Industries (Mundelein, IL) 1976-82, radios and phonographs; Justin Products, Inc. (NYC) 1984, radios; Kenner Products Co. (Cincinnati, OH) 1959, juke box phonograph; Noblitt-Sparks Industries, Inc. (Columbus, IN) 1938-41, radios; Porter Chemical Company (Hagerstown, MD) 1968, phonographs; Spears Products, Inc. (Bridgeport, CT) 1946-49, 58-61; Radio Corp. of America — RCA (NYC) 1951-53; Tiger Electronics, Inc. (Mundelein, IL) 1982, cassette tape player; and Vanity Fair Electronics Corp. (Brooklyn, NY) 1955-56, phonographs.

R2800 RECIPES

Cramer-Tobias-Meyer produced a series of recipe folder envelope stuffer using the Dwarfs from Snow White (also menus) in 1938. The American Dairy Assn. did a full Snow White Dairy Recipes book in 1955. In 1945 the Disney Studio provided the art for a fund raising program for L.A.'s Children's Hospital Convalescent Home called "The 60 Recipe Club". Each month subscribers received a 4" x 6" Disney character card and five recipes that best fit the current month. The recipes were supplied by movie or sports stars, political leaders, and other personalities. Each had an autograph reproduction. Donald Duck was featured in The 60 Recipe Club logo. The Mickey Mouse bread card promotion, beginning in 1933, was the largest use of recipes (see BREAD CARDS AND PREMIUMS).

R1005

R1008

R1006

R1008

R1010

R1006

R1025

Walt Disney's Snow White Dairy Recipes
Fun for the Whole Family

R2800

Dopey Just Ate Some of Snow White's Marvelous CHICKEN CURRY!

"OH, BOY! Spice Roll..."

R2800

R2800

R2800

R2800

R1000

R3005

R3015

R3016

R3020

R3022

R3070

R3072

R3085

R3024   R3026

R3020

R3000 RECORDS — PHONOGRAPH

Disney recorded music, film soundtracks, storyteller, educational, theme park and other recordings is a vast collecting area into itself. There are picture discs, albums with "pop-up" scenes, albums combined with books and all the different formats of recording technology from 78 RPM to digital audio. There isn't space to list everything, but the material presented is representative. Recording and distribution rights were sold to major labels until 1955. The Walt Disney Music Co. began in 1956 to produce soundtracks and records from the Mickey Mouse Club, releasing titles on Disneyland Record and Buena Vista Record labels. Exceptions have been promotional albums such as "The Greatest Hits of Walt Disney" and the fantastic Ovation Records Anthology of Classic Disney Art and Music, including a 52 page book on the history of Disney recorded music. (A 7" promotional preview of this album was made). Records have also been packaged with dolls, watches and other products. The *Pete's Dragon* soundtrack was released on Capitol Records. A few other more recent titles have been released on outside labels.

R3005

R3005	Mickey Mouse or Silly Symphony picture discs (RCA) 1933-38, each	50 - 350

RCA Victor Record Albums (R3015-R3049)

R3015	Snow White, 3 78 rpm records in illustrated envelope	20 - 100
R3016	Pinocchio 78 rpm (RCA)	15 - 65
R3020	Dumbo 78 rpm	15 - 65
R3022	Bambi	10 - 40
R3024	Snow White in hardcover album, 78 rpm	6 - 35
R3025	Snow White 45 rpm (different cover)	5 - 25
R3026	Peter and the Wolf	5 - 30
R3028	The Three Little Pigs	6 - 30
R3032	Johnny Appleseed	6 - 30
R3033	Pecos Bill	6 - 35
R3035	Cinderella, 78 or 45 rpm	5 - 25
R3036	Treasure Island	5 - 18
R3039	Peter Pan	5 - 25
R3045	Lady and the Tramp	5 - 20
R3049	Davy Crockett	4 - 15

Capitol Records (R3050-R3069)

R3050	Mickey and the Beanstalk, 78 rpm	5 - 25
R3052	Uncle Remus, 78 rpm	5 - 20

R3028

R3036

R3035

R3025

R3073

R3088

R3035

R3039

R3033

R3032

R3060

R3055

R3050

R3062

R3094

R3071

R3052

R3070

Spin and Marty. Value 3 - 12.

R3080

R3501

R3076

R3095

R3096

R3097

R3055	Little Toot, 78 rpm	5 - 18
R3060	So Dear To My Heart, 78 rpm	5 - 25
R3062	Robin Hood, 78 rpm	5 - 20
R3065	Lady and the Tramp, 45 rpm	4 - 15
R3069	Davy Crockett	4 - 15

Decca Records (R3070-R3079)

R3070	Snow White, 78, 45, or 33-1/3 rpm	5 - 25
R3071	Pinocchio, 78 rpm	10 - 40
R3072	Saludos Amigos, 78 rpm	5 - 25
R3073	The Three Caballeros, 78 rpm	5 - 20
R3076	Songs from Lady and the Tramp, 33-1/3 rpm	5 - 20
R3079	Davy Crockett	4 - 15
R3080	Alice in Wonderland premium records (2)	5 - 20

Columbia Records (R3085-R3099)

R3085	The Whale Who Wanted to Sing at the Met, 78 rpm	7 - 40
R3088	Bongo 78 rpm	5 - 25
R3094	Ballad of Davy Crockett, 78 rpm	4 - 15
R3095	Davy Crockett, Indian Fighter, 45 rpm	4 - 15
R3096	Davy Crockett Goes to Congress, 45 rpm	4 - 15
R3097	Davy Crockett at the Alamo, 45 rpm	4 - 15
R3099	Songs from the Magic Kingdom	3 - 12
R3200	Little Golden Records	

Little Golden Records were produced by Simon & Schuster in 78 and eventually 45 rpm. Some 33-1/3 speed records were produced in the 50's, but no Disney titles. Disney titles began with a separate numbering system, but were merged with the regular one somewhere between 100-200, even though the identifying "D" was retained as a preface. Mitch Miller and the Sandpipers were the talent on the first 100 or so records. Only records in jackets are considered collectible. Most sell in the 1 - 5 range.

R3200

R3200

R3200

R3200

R3525

R4211

R3551

R4200

R4210

R3620

R4090

R4093

R3600

R4075

68

R3500 Disneyland and Buena Vista Records, Disney's own labels, produced a small number of 78 rpm records. They did a
number of 45 rpm singles, but put a major production effort in the
long playing 33-1/3 speed that was to become the standard of
children's records. Ads in the 1956 issues of *Mickey Mouse Club*
magazine show attractively designed covers for the major Disney
classics featuring the original film soundtracks. Soon thereafter,
the record and book versions appeared. Around 1963 a short
series of "Pop-up Panorama Storybook" albums were issued. New
45 rpm storybook albums came along in the 60's and have become
a regular product category for each new film. Cassette tape
versions of the same storybooks were added in the 70's.

R3501 Mickey Mouse Club, 45 or 78 rpm, each	1 - 8
R3525 Annette titles	3 - 15
R3550 33-1/3 LP Albums, 50's	1 - 15
R3551 Other 45 rpm records or albums, 50's or 60's	1 - 8
R3600 LP Albums, 60's (except pop-up)	1 - 8
R3620 Pop-up albums with 4 complete pop-up scenes. Titles include *Dumbo* and *Sword in the Stone,* each	10 - 50
R3700 LP Albums 70's and 80's	1 - 5
R3701 45 rpm records or albums 70's or 80's	1 - 3

The Disney labels have also released albums for many of their
theme park attractions. Most remain available, but some were
withdrawn due to attraction or other changes.

R3900 Theme park albums in current release	1 - 7
R3950 Withdrawn theme park records	2 - 20
R4000 Premium albums	2 - 15
R4050 Special anniversary albums	2 - 15
R4075 Picture discs, Snow White, Pinocchio, Cinderella, Lady and the Tramp, Mary Poppins, Fox and the Hound, or Mickey's Christmas Carol, each	1 - 6
R4090 America on Parade (See A4000)	5 - 50
R4091 Walt Disney World Electric Water Pageant (1973)	5 - 15
R4092 Disney's Main Street Electrical Parade	1 - 3
R4093 A Musical Souvenir of Walt Disney World's Magic Kingdom	1 - 7
R4200 Ronco's The Greatest Hits of Walt Disney with uncut cutouts and song sheets	10 - 25
R4200 Record and jacket only	2 - 8

R3701

R4092

R4215

Casette tape. Value 1 - 5.

R3700

R4075

69

R5020

R6008

R6006   R6007   R6005

R6010

R8700

R7025   R7010

R8700

R4210 The Magical Music of Walt Disney with book   20 - 50
R4211 Promotional sampler for R4210   2 - 10
R4215 Show 'n Tell record and film strip (GE), each   1 - 3
Licensed manufacturers — Capitol Records (Hollywood, CA) 1947-55; Columbia Records (NYC) 1946-47, 55; Decca Distributing Corp. and Decca Records, Inc. (NYC) 1947-55; Disneyland Record Co. (NYC) 1956-85; General Electric Co. (Utica, NY) 1970-71; Ovation Records (Glenview, IL) 1978; RCA Victor Corp. (Camden, NJ) 1933-55; Ronco Teleproducts Inc. (Elk Grove Village, IL) 1976; and Simon & Schuster (NYC) 1949-58, Little Golden Records.

R5000 RINGS

The earliest Mickey ring on record was made by Cohn & Rosenberger in 1931. Brier Mfg. distributed rings in the mid to late 30's. Ostby & Barton sterling silver rings were sold beginning in 1947 and also packaged with some Ingersoll watches of the same period. There have been a number of premium rings and the theme parks prompted a proliferation of souvenir rings.

R5005 Mickey (Cohn & Rosenberger)   15 - 75
R5010 Mickey, Donald or Dopey (Brier)   10 - 50
R5020 Mickey, Donald, Pluto, Bongo or Bambi (pastel or luminous background), oval or square, each   8 - 35
R5032 Hardy Boys ring (International Shoe) premium   8 - 25
R5038 Snow White ring (1972)   2 - 10
R5040 Donald Duck "Living Toy" ring (Kellogg's Pep) 1949   15 - 40
R5041 Pinocchio ring   15 - 40
R5042 Sword in the Stone ring (plastic)   10 - 20
R5100 Theme park, character souvenir, cloisonne   1 - 10
R5101 Theme parks, logo souvenirs   1 - 8
R5102 Same as R5100 only silver   2 - 20
R5103 Character ring, souvenir, metal   1 - 4
R5110 Sam the Olympic Eagle, plastic   1 - 2
Licensed manufacturers — Benay-Albee Novelty Co. (Maspeth, NY) 1972; Brier Mfg. Co. (Providence, RI) 1935-42, 55; Childstar, Ltd. (NYC) 1974-84; Cohn & Rosenberger (NYC) 1931-36, 41-42; Dexter Mfg. Co. (Providence, RI) 1953, 56, 68-83; International Shoe Co. (St. Louis) 1957; Kellogg Company (Battle Creek, MI) 1949; and Ostby & Barton Co. (Providence, RI) 1947-49, Osbee rings.
Also see — JEWELRY

R6000 ROCKING HORSES, BOUNCE, SPRING ACTION AND OTHER PLAY EQUIPMENT

The Mengel Co. created several different ways to rock and ride Mickey and Snow White. Pontiac Spring and Bumper Co. developed four different characters to bounce on. There were also Fantasia unicorns, Mickey see-saws, Mickey slides and other outdoor play equipment.

R6004 Mickey large head hobby horse (Borgfeldt)   60 - 300
R6005 Mickey rocking horse (Mengel)   50 - 250
R6006 Mickey shoofly rocker (Mengel)   60 - 300
R6007 Mickey riding swing (Mengel)   60 - 300
R6008 Mickey folding 8' slide (Mengel)   25 - 75
R6010 Spring action bounce toy, Mickey, Donald, Pluto or Dopey (Pontiac Spring)   40 - 175
B6050 FANTASIA unicorn outdoor bounce toy   10 - 50
Licensed manufacturers — Geo Borgfeldt & Co. (NYC) 1931-41; The Mengel Co. (St. Louis, MO) 1935-39; Miracle Recreation Eqpt. Co. (Grinnell, IW) 1973-84, backyard play equipment; Pontiac Spring and Bumper Co. aka Hugh Chalmers Jr. (Pontiac, MI) 1937-40; Tennessee Valley Associates (Nashville, TN) 1943-45, Shoo Fly rocking chairs and rocking horses; and Wonder Products Company — subsidiary of Wilson Sporting Goods (Collierville, TN) 1972.

R7000 ROLY-POLYS

Roly-poly toys have a round weighted bottom to keep their figures upright even as baby tries to knock them over. They are often musical.

R7010 Mickey on ball (Borgfeldt)   50 - 175
R7025 Dopey, head or full figure (Crown)   12 - 60
P7075 Mickey, Donald, or Pluto (Gund)   5 - 18
Licensed manufacturers — Geo. Borgfeldt & Co. (NYC) 1931-41; Crown Toy Mfg. Co. (Brooklyn, NY) 1937-41; Gund Mfg. Co. (NYC) 1947-55, 59, 68-71; and Plastic Playthings, Inc. (White Plains, NY) 1952-58.

R8700 RUB-ON TRANSFERS

Colorforms has made a pie-eye Mickey transfer set that looks

WALT DISNEY character rings by osbee
STERLING SILVER $1.00 ADJUSTABLE SIZES

R5005
R5040
R5010
R5038
R5020

R5005   R5010   R5020

R5020   R5103   R5100

R5103   R5110

Mickey Mouse RUGS

R9000

S1520

Lithographed

METAL TOYS

With the Three Little Pigs and Big Bad Wolf

Tea sets up to 23 pieces, garden sets, laundry sets, sand pails, shovels, drums—virtually every plaything idea has been developed in finest quality lithographed metal with full color illustrations of Disney subjects. Children are seeing this merchandise everywhere and sales have reached the highest level in all our experience.

Write for illustrated folder giving all particulars. This merchandise has year-round sales appeal. Cash in on it now!

Write for full particulars

OHIO ART COMPANY

Licensee

Bryan, Ohio

New York Sales Office   200 Fifth Ave., New York

Lithographed Metal

PLAYTHINGS

with colorful Mickey Mouse designs

Tea sets, sand pails, garden sets, sprinklers, snow shovels, metal drums beautifully lithographed in many colors and manufactured to meet a very great popular-priced market.

The fascinating scenes taken from Mickey Mouse Motion picture films have increased the sales appeal to the point where competition does not exist.

Write for full particulars

OHIO ART COMPANY

Licensee

Bryan, Ohio

New York Sales Office—200 Fifth Ave.

S1545

S1540

S1510

S1511

S1522

S1529   S1528   S1527   S1526 S1525

72

old but is not. The wax release transfers became widely used in the 70's as premiums in Jiffy Pop popcorn and in various activity sets. Kept but not really collected, these items bring only .50 - 2.

R9000 RUGS, TAPESTRIES AND MATS

Mickey Mouse area rugs and tapestries have been made since 1935. If the piece is velvety, it is likely old. Beware of newer, yet dirty, carpets being sold as old. Character carpets come as large as 6' x 9'. Most, however are around 2-1/2' x 4'. Value on the 30's velvet like examples range from 35 - 250. Newer area rugs sell for 8 - 45.

Licensed manufacturers — Alagold Products (Montgomery, AL) 1982-83, foam-cusioned vinyl resting mat; Jorges Carpet Mills, Inc. (Rossville, GA) 1976-80, carpets featuring children's games; Joy Carpets (Ft. Oglethorpe, GA) 1982, Race to the Magic Kingdom game carpet; Lysander Tufted products division of Eli L. Sandler & Co. (NYC) 1971-72, scatter rugs and textile wall hangings; The Malloy Co. (Philadelphia, PA) 1970-71, polyure-thane bath mats; Quetta Carpet Sales Ltd. — Rugby Rugs, Inc. (NYC) 1976-77, area rugs; Sandura Co., Inc. (Philadelphia, PA) 1940-42, floor covering; Shillcraft — A & H Shillman Co., Inc. (Baltimore, MD) 1972-84, rug kits; and Alexander Smith & Sons Carpet Co. (Yonkers, NY) 1935-37, wool, cotton or jute carpets and rugs.

S1000 SALT AND PEPPER SHAKERS

There were some 30's Mickey china salt and peppers made in Germany and Japan. Plastic Novelties was authorized to make them in 1935 and a J. L. Wright metal set — Sneezy and Dopey — was made in 1938. The largest producer was Leeds China. Dan Brechner made a number of sets and Disney theme parks have sold souvenir sets.

S1015	Mickey china salt and pepper in holder	50 - 250
S1025	Sneezy/Dopey, metal (J. L. Wright)	20 - 60
S1040	Mickey/Minnie (Leeds)	6 - 15
S1041	Donald/Donald (Leeds)	5 - 15
S1042	Dumbo/Dumbo 2-1/2" (Leeds)	5 - 12
S1043	Dumbo/Dumbo 4" (Leeds)	8 - 20
S1044	Pluto/Pluto (Leeds)	5 - 12
S1045	Thumper/Thumper (Leeds)	5 - 12
S1060	Mickey/Mickey (Brechner)	4 - 12
S1061	Donald/Donald (Brechner)	4 - 12
S1062	Ludwig Von Drake/Donald (Brechner)	4 - 12
S1063	Mickey/Minnie on bench (Brechner)	4 - 15
S1064	Snow White/Dopey (Enesco)	5 - 20
S1075	Dwarf heads	2 - 10
S1100	Mickey/Minnie heads, glass jar	2 - 8
S1110	Mickey salad maker, ceramic pie-eyes	2 - 6

Licensed manufacturers — Dan Brechner & Co., Inc. (NYC) 1961-63; Enesco Imports, Inc. (Chicago) 1968-72; Leeds China Co. (Chicago) 1944-54; Plastic Novelties, Inc. (NYC) 1935-55; and J. L. Wright (Chicago) 1938-39.

S1500 SAND BOX TOYS, SAND PAILS AND LITHO METAL SHOVELS

Ohio Art Company has been the major producer of Disney lithographed material toys since 1933. Sand pails, shovels, water-ing cans and sand sifters, were made in a variety of sizes picturing Mickey, Minnie, Donald, Pluto, the Three Pigs, Snow White and the 7 Dwarfs. Many Ohio Art pieces in the late 30's are dated. J. Chein & Co. made litho metal sand pails in the 50's and 60's. Eldon Mfg. Company made plastic sets starting in 1955. The slightest rust has dramatic negative impact on value.

Ohio Art Company (S1510-S1545)

S1510	Ohio Art sand sets in box, includes sprinkling can, small bucket and litho shovel with Disney characters, plus sand mold and scoop, in box	50 - 250
S1511	Same as S1510, but no sprinkling can	35 - 210
S1512	Same as S1510, but includes sand elevator	60 - 275
S1513	Same as S1510, but includes sand sifter	75 - 325
S1520	Litho shovels, single piece litho metal, 2 sizes	15 - 50
S1521	Litho shovels, wooden handle	25 - 100
S1522	Litho snow shovels	55 - 150
S1525	Sand pails, 3" to 3-1/2" tall, each	8 - 25
S1526	Sand pails, 4" tall, each	10 - 35
S1527	Sand pails, 5" tall, each	15 - 55
S1528	Sand pails, 8" to 10", each	25 - 75
S1529	Sand pails, 12" or more	50 - 200
S1535	Sand sifter, 6" diameter	15 - 40

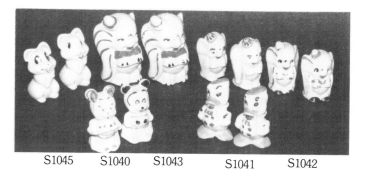

S1045 S1040 S1043 S1041 S1042

S1512

S1541 S1542 S1536

S1110

S1075   S1062   S1063   S1061   S1064

S1521

S1700

S2005

EIGHT ASSORTED COLORS

MICKEY MOUSE

COLORED PENCILS

DIXON

P1311

YooHoo! HAVE A MICKEY MOUSE ICE CREAM CONE

MICKEY MOUSE and his friends

S2120

MICKEY MOUSE

COMPOSITION BOOK

S2005

DOPEY NOTE BOOK

S2060

White and Wyckoff 1938 school supplies and stationery. Value 10 - 45 each.

S1536	Sand sifter, 7-1/2″ diameter	15 - 40
S1540	Sprinkling cans, 3″ tall, each	8 - 25
S1541	Sprinkling cans, 4″ - 4-1/2″ tall, each	10 - 35
S1542	Sprinkling cans, 6″ tall or larger	12 - 55
S1545	Sand sifter set with scoop and molds	25 - 75
S1650	Chein sand pails	10 - 35
S1700	Eldon sand mold sets, each	5 - 18

Licensed manufacturers — J. Chein & Co., Inc. (NYC) 1955, 68; Eldon Mfg. Co. (LA) 1955; Harwood Co. (Farmingdale, NJ) 1970, plastic pails with shovels; Ohio Art Co. (Bryan, OH) 1933-42, 44-45, 82; and Worcester Toy Co. division of Plascor, Inc. (Worcester, MA) 1972-79.

S2000 SCHOOL SUPPLIES

Walt Disney once recalled the first time he was ever paid for the use of Mickey Mouse on merchandise. He was in New York, and an unknown man sought him out at his hotel and gave Walt $300 cash to use his characters on school supplies. The first actual licenses were issued to the Powers Paper Company and American Lithographic Co. in 1931. Disney characters have appeared on school supplies almost continuously ever since.

S2005	Powers Paper binders, composition books, tablets, stationery, and drawing tablets copyright by Walt Disney, values vary widely depending on completeness, condition, amount of writing and graphics, each	5 - 100
S2060	Powers Paper, main characters, Copyright Walt Disney Enterprises (see S2005), each	5 - 85
S2090	Powers, Snow White characters (see S2005), each	5 - 65
S2112	Pinocchio character, each	5 - 75
S2120	Mickey Mouse ice cream cone ruler	10 - 50
S2122	Tablets with Walt Disney Comics and Stories cover art, each	8 - 25
S2128	Tablets, win a trip to Disneyland, each	5 - 20
S2130	Pencil tablet with trading cards, each	5 - 20
S2131	Mickey Mouse Club scribble pads, each	3 - 10
S2133	Davy Crockett or Zorro, each	3 - 12
S2135	Tablets, notebook filler paper, folders or book covers, 60's, 70's or 80's	1 - 5
S2140	School bags, 40's or 50's	5 - 20
S2141	School bags, 60's, 70's or 80's	1 - 8

Licensed manufacturers — American Lithographic Co. (NYC) 1931, school tablets (may have been printer for Powers Paper); Cardinal Products division of Josten's Business Products, Inc. (Minneapolis, MN) 1982-83, vinyl binders, portfolios, pad holders and clipboards; Dasco Manufacturing Co., Inc. subsidiary of Pak-Well Corp. (Oakland, CA) 1973-79, composition books, looseleaf paper, binders, memo books and activity kits; Donald Art Co., Inc. (Mamaroneck, NY) 1950-51, school tablet covers; Feldco Loose Leaf Corp. (Chicago) 1949-50, binders, tablets and

S2005

S2112

S2090

S2090

S2122

S2140

S2135

S2130

S2135

S2128

S2305

S2307

S2315

S2135

other products; Gay-Craft (NYC) 1947-48; schoolbags and novelties; Alexander Miner Mfg. Co. (NYC) 1955-56, vinyl plastic toy school bag; National Leather Mfg. Co. (Brooklyn, NY) 1951-55, 68-70, school, utility and lunch bags; Al Nyman and Son, Inc. (NYC, then Miami, FL) 1972-84, full line of school supplies and bags; Pak-Well Corp. (see Dasco Mfg. Co.); Prudential-Feldco Inc. (Glendale, Queens, NY) 1979-84, composition books, looseleaf paper, binders/arrangers and memo books; Powers Paper Company (Springfield, MO) 1931-40, children's stationery and school supplies; and Western Tablet and Stationery Corp. (St. Joseph, MO) 1939-41, later Westab, Inc. 1968-74

S2131

S2200 SCISSORS

A pair of metal scissors with a litho metal 30's Mickey and a Donald Duck electric scissors set comprise the most collectible pieces in this class. A number of plastic character safety scissors have been made since the 50's.

S2210	Mickey metal scissors	10 - 50
S2225	Donald Duck electric scissors set	8 - 35
S2230	Plastic character scissors, post 1950	1 - 4

Licensed manufacturers — Kurlash Co. (Rochester, NY) 1937-39 plus Royal American Corp. and Universal Novelties Corp. (Chicago) 1947-49, Donald Duck electric scissors.

S2300 SCRAPBOOKS AND PHOTO ALBUMS

Whitman did a great Mickey/Minnie scrapbook in 1936, a Snow White version with the original movie poster art in 1938, and one from Pinocchio. There were a couple different Mickey Mouse Club scrapbook designs in 1956 and a 1977 version for the New Mickey Mouse Club. Photo albums were produced in the 50's in conjunction with the TV MMC. Theme parks produced a series of vinyl photo albums filled with photo scenes of each land.

S2135

S2304	Three Pigs (Krueger)	20 - 65
S2305	Mickey/Minnie	15 - 65
S2307	Snow White and the 7 Dwarfs	10 - 50
S2310	Pinocchio	15 - 65
S2315	Mickey Mouse Club designs (50's)	5 - 18
S2316	New Mickey Mouse Club (1977)	1 - 4
S2350	Photo albums (General Products), each	1 - 8
S2365	Theme park photo albums with photos, each	1 - 8

Licensed manufacturers — General Products of Chicago (Chicago) 1956-57; Richard G. Krueger, Inc. (NYC) 1931-41; and Whitman Publishing Co. (Racine, WI) 1933-85.

S2500 SEEDS AND BULBS

Two sets of seeds packets were sold by Germain Seed and Plant Company starting in 1937. The Snow White and the 7 Dwarfs packets were also offered by Swift and Company for 10¢ and Allsweet oleomargarine package ends. B. T. Babbett, Inc. offered a set of 8 Crocus bulbs in 1938 — a special marked white one for Snow White and seven purple ones for each of the Dwarfs.

S2230   S2225

S2510   S2506

S2505

77

PUMPKIN ZINNIA PEAS HOLLYHOCK DAISY

SUNFLOWER BEANS SQUASH CARROT MARIGOLD

SWEET CORN TOMATO LETTUCE CUCUMBER RADISH

S2570

S2515

S2870

S2880

A5016

S2815

S2832

AMSCO CORPORATION

"Snow White Sewing Set" #1529
Suggested retail price $2.00

Amsco Corporation
200 Fifth Avenue
New York, N. Y. 10010

Stitch-a-Picture Yarn Plaques
Suggested retail price $3.00

S3070

S3010

Colorforms issued 15 different seed packs in 1977 featuring 30's and early 40's style character art.

S2509

S2505	Mickey, Donald and Pluto, 3 pack	50 - 175
S2506	Mickey Mouse — Zinnia, Donald Duck — Cosmos or Pluto — Marigold, individual packs,	15 - 45
S2509	Snow White, Dwarfs and Wicked Queen, 3 pack	45 - 150
S2510	Snow White and the 7 Dwarfs — Collection of Dwarf flowers, Snow White and animals — Sweet Pea, or Wicked Queen — Zinnia, individual packs	12 - 40
S2515	Snow White and the 7 Dwarfs crocus set	35 - 85
S2570	Colorforms seed pack including plastic markers, each	1 - 4

Licensed manufacturers — B. T. Babbett, Inc. (NYC) 1938; Colorforms (Norwood, NJ) 1968-84; Germain Seed and Plant Co. (LA) 1937-40, same packets used in Swift Allsweet offer; Green America (see Colorforms); and Union Wadding Co., Inc. (Pawtucket, RI) 1970-82.

S2800 SEWING, NEEDLEWORK, EMBROIDERY, ETC.

In 1931 Vogue Needlecraft Co. made 12 or so different designs for pillow tops, dresser scarfs, crib sets, aprons, shoe and laundry bags, card table covers and other uses. The lining is marked Copyright Walt Disney. Marks Brothers introduced two sizes of sewing cards in 1934. The supply of sets, kits, and books has been steady to present date. Soreng-Manegold produced yarn holders and lamps with identical bases. The lamps, however, are not yarn dispensers.

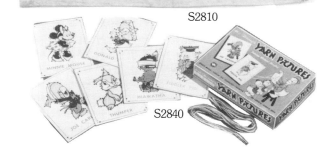

S2810	Vogue needlecraft sets, each	5 - 55
S2815	Sewing set (Marks Bros.) 2 sizes, each	10 - 75
S2820	Yarn holder (Soreng-Manegold) green or tan	8 - 22
S2832	Walt Disney Character embroidery set (Standard Toykraft)	12 - 55
S2840	Yarn Pictures (Jaymar) 1946 or 47	10 - 35
S2846	Lady and the Tramp embroidery set (Highland)	5 - 15
S2848	Davy Crockett art needlework sets (Ulmann)	5 - 18
S2870	Paragon cross stitch kits and book	2 - 12
S2871	Whitman sewing card sets (began in 1970)	1 - 8
S2880	Walt Disney characters needlepoint book	1 - 10
S2885	Mickey Mouse Sew-Ons (Colorforms)	1 - 4
S2890	Minnie Mouse sewing kit (Walt Disney World and Disneyland Hotels) 1971-85	.50 - 1

Licensed manufacturers — Chicago Art Needle Works Co. (Chicago) 1938-39; Colorforms (Norwood, NJ) 1968-84; Highland Art Embroidery Co. (Pasadena, CA) 1953-55, toy embroidery sets; Jaymar Specialty Co. (NYC) 1947-84; Marks Brothers Co. (Boston) 1934-41, 46-48; Mazaltov's Inc. (Amityville, NY) 1975-79, needlepoint kits; Murry Hill Products, Inc. (NYC) 1968, sewing kit assortments; Notions, Inc. (NYC) 1938-39; Paragon Art and Linen Co., Inc. (Bronx, NY) 1970-71, then National Paragon Corp. (NYC) 1974-84; Peri-Lusta, Ltd. (Bronx, NY) 1972-73, art needlework kits; RLW Embroidery Corp. (Union City, NJ) 1948-49, embroidered materials; Soreng-Manegold Co. (Chicago) 1934-38, sewing kits and yarn holders; Standard Toykraft Products (NYC) 1939-41; Bernard Ulmann Co., Inc. (Long Island City, NY) 1953-59, unfinished art needlework; Vogue Needlecraft Co. (NYC) 1931-32; Whitman Publishing Co. (Racine, WI) 1933-85; and Yankee Homecraft Corp. (East Natick, MA) 1968, "Knit-Wit" Knits.

S3000 EVAN K. SHAW COMPANY

Evan K. Shaw was the successor to or always owned the American Pottery Company. The company also purchased the Vernon Kiln Company or just its molds. Exactly how all this took place, or when, is the subject of conflicting data. Labeled pieces found indicate ceramic figures once sold as American Pottery were advertised later by and have been marked Shaw. New Shaw figures were also marketed under the American Pottery and the Poppytrail names, presumably to allow the company to offer exclusive lines to competing major market department stores ... or other outlets where these ceramic art figures were traditionally sold. The initial figures are listed at American Pottery (see A5000). The exclusively Shaw pieces seem to start with The Three Caballeros (1945-46) even though the record shows the license to be in the name of American Pottery Co. at 527 W. 7th Street, Los Angeles from 1943-50 and in the name of Evan K. Shaw at the same address for the years 1951-55. Lady and the Tramp figures were the last Disney ones produced by the company. Stan Pawl-

S3026

S2810

S2840

S3063   S3060   S3067   S3061

S2885

S3105

S3104

S3014

S3045   S3040   S3047   S3043

S3110

owski helped with information and photos from his collection used in presenting this section. Prices are a composite sample, and should be weighed on the up side on the West Coast.

S3010	Donald, Jose or Panchito (1946), each	40 - 100
S3014	Dumbo, standing or sitting up (1946), each	40 - 125
S3016	Stork or Crow from Dumbo (1946), each	50 - 155
S3020	Pinocchio or Jiminy Cricket (1946), each	55 - 200
S3022	Figaro, 2 running, 1 seated (1946), each	30 - 65
S3026	Pluto, 4 different poses (1946), each	20 - 50
S3030	Bambi, prone or Owl, each	25 - 75
S3032	Planters, Br'er Rabbit, Thumper or Owl on stump, each	25 - 65
S3034	Planters, Donald in boat or Pluto in doghouse, each	40 - 80
S3040	Cinderella in rags	50 - 155
S3041	Cinderella or Prince dressed for the ball, each	45 - 150
S3043	Bruno, sitting or prone, each	35 - 115
S3045	Gus or Jaq, each	35 - 115
S3047	Bluebirds, mama mouse or baby mouse, each	20 - 65
S3060	Alice in Wonderland	50 - 700
S3061	Tweedle Dee or Tweedle Dum, each	35 - 150
S3063	Walrus, March Hare, White Rabbit or Mad Hatter, each	35 - 150
S3067	Dormouse	30 - 90
S3070	Teapots, 4 different, each	50 - 185
S3080	Fantasia and other figures from Vernon Kiln molds, hippo, elephant, unicorn, sprites, and Hop-Lo mushroom salt and pepper	20 - 140

S3080 Fantasia and other figures from Vernon Kiln molds, hippo, elephant, unicorn, sprites, and Hop-Lo mushroom salt and pepper shakers, valued 10% to 20% below original versions, see VERNON KILNS.

S3090 Small versions were made of many Dumbo, Three Caballeros, Bambi, Pinocchio and main character figures. These are rarer. Some have been reported as being made in Mexico under a different license. Some appear on U. S. catalog sheets. While more scarce, they lack color and detail. Some collectors feel they are worth more, others feel they are not as valuable as art. The buyer can be his own judge on these.

S4000	Peter Pan, sitting or standing	25 - 100
S4002	Tinker Bell or Mermaid, each	25 - 100
S4004	Wendy, Michael, or Nana, each	20 - 75
S4010	Lady and the Tramp figures, Lady (sitting or standing), Tramp, Peg, Si, Am, Jock, Trusty, Limey, Dachsie, Fluffy, Ruffles, Scooter, or Scamp, each	15 - 45

S3100 SHEET MUSIC, FOLIOS AND MUSIC BOOKS

Sheet music is collected for cover art and for the music. The covers on music from cartoons or shorts are unique to each song. The animated features usually had a single design for all the different pieces published for the film, only the song title at the top of the sheet changed. Exceptions include Honest John, Jiminy Cricket, and Monstro the Whale from *Pinocchio* and all the sheets from *Bambi* (each used a different character in a second colon with *Bambi* as part of the same basic design). The Mickey Mouse Club "Theme Song" (Minnie's Yoo Hoo) member's edition was probably the first music published and was later released in illustrated sheet music form. "Mickey Mouse (You Cute Little Fellow)" was published in the first Mickey Mouse book by Bibo & Lang in 1930. There have been premium and giveaway music sheets and folios; music store folios and music books; special song books included with musical instruments such as the Magnus organ and Mousegetars. Various music publishers handled the rights over the years until the company formed the Walt Disney Music Company (Oct 1949). The new company published non-Disney music for a time, one of the most notable hits being Frankie Laine's "Mule Train". Nearly all music folios are illustrated with scenes from the films in which they originated. Theme park attractions and TV shows have also been a source of printed music. A special music promotion program at Disneyland resulted in a Music Education Program teacher's guide. Early sheet music published by Irving Berlin is more valuable than later editions published by Bourne.

S3102 Mickey Mouse Club "Theme Song" — Minnie's

S3041

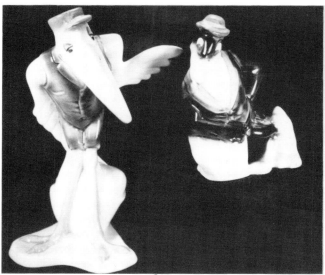
S3016

S3143

S3102

S3116

S3125

S3112

S3111

S3130

S3135

S3114

S3113

S3153

S3290

	Yoo Hoo (1929-30)	10 - 40
S3103	"Minnie's Yoo Hoo" — music store version (1930)	50 - 250
S3104	"The Wedding Party of Mickey Mouse" (1931)	35 - 150
S3105	"What? No Mickey Mouse? (What Kind of a Party is This?)" 1932	35 - 150
S3107	"Mickey Mouse and Minnie's in Town" (1933)	20 - 70
S3108	"Lullaby Land" (1933)	15 - 50
S3109	"Dance of the Bogey Man" (1933)	15 - 50
S3110	"Who's Afraid of the Big Bad Wolf?" (1933)	7 - 18
S3111	"The World Owes Me a Living" (Grasshopper and the Ants) 1934	10 - 40
S3112	"You're Nothin' but a Nothin'" (The Flying Mouse) 1934	10 - 40
S3113	Silly Symphony Folio (1934)	10 - 50
S3114	"Mickey Mouse's Birthday Party" (1936)	15 - 55
S3115	"Mickey Mouse and Silly Symphony" Folio (1936)	10 - 40
S3116	Songs from Snow White and the Seven Dwarfs (1937-38) — (Irving Berlin) "Bluddle-Uddle-Um-Dum", "The Silly Song" (The Dwarfs Yodel Song), "Heigh-Ho", "I'm Wishing", "One Song", "Snow White", "Some Day My Prince Will Come", "Whistle While You Work" or "With a Smile and a Song", each	5 - 15
S3125	Snow White Souvenir Albums (2) Bourne, each	10 - 25
S3128	Snow White folio (England version)	10 - 30
S3130	"Ferdinand the Bull" (1938)	8 - 20
S3135	Songs from Pinocchio (1939-40) — "Give A Little Whistle", "Hi-Diddle-Dee-Dee", "I've Got No Strings", "Little Wooden Head", "Three Cheers for Anything", "Turn on the Old Music Box" or "When You Wish Upon a Star", each	6 - 18
S3143	Special cover Pinocchio songs — "Figaro and Cleo", "Honest John", "Jiminy Cricket" or "Monstro the Whale"	12 - 45
S3147	Souvenir Album of Songs from Pinocchio (Bourne)	8 - 36
S3148	The Nutcracker Suite (Fantasia) 1940	10 - 50
S3150	The Reluctant Dragon (1941)	10 - 40
S3153	Dumbo Song Book (premium)	3 - 20
S3154	Songs from Dumbo (1941) — "Baby Mine", "Casey Junior", "Look Out For Mister Stork", "Pink Elephants on Parade", "Song of the Roustabouts" or "When I See an Elephant Fly", each	10 - 20
S3160	Songs from Bambi — "Lets Sing a Gay Little Spring Song", "Little April Shower", "Looking for Romance (I Bring You a Song)", "Love is a Song", "Thumper Song", or "Twitterpated", each	8 - 18
S3168	Songs from Saludos Amigos — "Brazil (Aquarela do Brazil)" or "Saludos Amigos", each	5 - 10
S3170	"Der Fuehrer's Face" (1942)	10 - 35
S3171	"Hop on Your Pogo Stick" (1942) Victory Vehicles	10 - 40
S3172	"The Yankee Doodle Spirit" (1942) The New Spirit	10 - 40
S3175	Songs from Walt Disney Pictures (1943) folio	8 - 20
S3178	Songs of Victory Through Air Power (1943) — "Song of the Eagle" or "The Victory March", each	15 - 75
S3180	Songs of The Three Caballeros (1945-46) — "Angel-May-Care", "Baia", Mexico", title song, "You Belong to My Heart" or "Jesusita en Chihuahua", each	4 - 8
S3184	The Three Caballeros (Peer Music) folio (1944)	8 - 20
S3188	Songs from Make Mine Music (1945-46) — "All the Cats Join In", "Blue Bayou", "Casey, the Pride of Them All", "Johnny Fedora and Alice Blue Bonnet", "Make Mine Music", "Two Silhouettes" or "Without You", each	3 - 8
S3297	Pinocchio: Souvenir Album or Snow White Fantasy (Bourne) 1945, each	5 - 15
S3200	Songs of Song of the South — "Everybody Has a Laughing Place", "How Do You Do?", "Song of the South", "Sooner or Later", "Uncle Remus Said" or "Zip-A-Dee-Doo-Dah", each	3 - 8
S3208	Songs of Fun and Fancy Free — "Beanero",	

S3115

S3154

S3172 S3178 S3171   S3168

S3175

S3160

S3180

S3188

S3200

S3208

S3219

S3225

S3230

S3235

S3245

S3255

S3283

"Fee-Fi-Fo-Fum", "Fun and Fancy Free", "Happy
Go Lucky Fellow", "Lazy Countryside", "My
Favorite Dream", "My What a Happy Day",
"Say It With a Slap" or "Too Good to Be
True", each 3 - 8

S3218 "Trick or Treat" (1948) cartoon 8 - 22

S3219 Songs of *Melody Time* (1948) — "Apple Song",
"Blame It on the Samba", "Blue Shadows on the
Trail", "Little Toot", "The Lord is Good to Me",
"Once Upon A Wintertime", "Melody Time",
"Pecos Bill", "The Pioneer Song", each 4 - 10

S3225 Songs of *So Dear To My Heart* (1948) — "The
County Fair", "It's Whatcha Do With Whatcha
Got", "Lavender Blue (Dilly Dilly)", "So Dear
to My Heart", "Stick-to-it-ivity", each 3 - 8

S3230 Songs from *The Adventures of Ichabod and Mr.
Toad* (1949) — The Headless Horseman",
"Ichabod", "Katrina" or "The Merrily Song", each 8 - 22

S3235 Songs from *Cinderella* (1948-50) — "Bibbidi-
Bobbidi-Boo", "Cinderella", "A Dream is a Wish
Your Heart Makes", "Oh Sing, Sweet Nightingale",
"So This Is Love" or "The Work Song", each 4 - 10

S3242 *Cinderella* folio (1949) 5 - 12

S3244 "Jing-A-Ling, Jing-A-Ling" *(Beaver Valley)* 1950 4 - 10

S3245 Songs from *Alice in Wonderland* (1949-51) — "I'm
Late", "'Twas Brillig", "The Unbirthday Song",
"Very Good Advice", "March of the Cards",
"Alice in Wonderland", "In a World of My
Own", "How D'ye Do and Shake Hands" or "All
In the Golden Afternoon", each 4 - 10

S3255 Songs from *Peter Pan* (1951) — "The Elegant
Captain Hook", "Never Smile at a Crocodile",
"Peter Pan", "The Second Star to the Right
(Off to Never Land)", "What Made the Red
Man Red", "You Can Fly" or "Your Mother
and Mine", each 4 - 10

S3265 Themes from *The Living Desert* — "The
Desert Blooms", "Kangaroo Rat" and "The
Living Desert", All on same sheet, each 5 - 12

S3275 Songs from *Lady and the Tramp* (1952-55) —
"Bella Notte", "He's A Tramp", "Lady",
"La-La-Lu", "Peace On Earth", or "Siamese Cat
Song", each 4 - 10

S3280 "The Ballad of Davy Crockett" (1954) 5 - 12

S3283 Disneyland Music Books (Hansen Publications)
1955, titles include — *The Ballad of Davy
Crockett, Bambi, Cinderella, Alice in
Wonderland, Fantasia — The Nutcracker Suite,
or Peter Pan*, each 5 - 10

S3289 Mickey Mouse March 6 - 15

S3290 Mouseketunes (Song book for a Mousegetar) 3 - 10

S3291 "Davy Crockett King of the Wild Frontier" (1955) 5 - 12

S3292 "Davy Crockett and the River Pirates" 5 - 12

S3295 Theme from *Zorro* (1957) 5 - 10

S3300 Songs from *Sleeping Beauty* (1952-59) — "I
Wonder", "Love Theme", "Once Upon A
Dream", "Sing A Smiling Song", or "Sleeping
Beauty", each 5 - 10

S3310 *Mary Poppins* sheet music or song books, each 3 - 7

S3330 Walt Disney music song book (1960-84) 1 - 8

S3340 The Illustrated Disney Song Book 5 - 18

S3360 Disneyland's Music Education Program teacher's
guide 3 - 12

S3362 Sherman Brothers Bicentennial song 1 - 4

Licensed publishers — Bourne, Inc. (NYC) 1947-48; Broadcast Music
(NYC) 1942-53; Hansen Publications (NYC) 1955; Irving Berlin, Inc.
(NYC) 1933-41; Irving Caesar (NYC) 1932-33; Leeds Music Corp. (NYC)
1946-51, music books; Magnus Organ Corp. (Woodbury, NY) 1974-75,
organ songbook; Santly-Joy, Inc. (NYC) 1946-48; and Southern Music
Publishing Co. (NYC) 1942-50.

S3400 SHEETS, PILLOWS,
BEDSPREADS AND DRAPES

Products in this classification have been produced since 1933.
Designs have been proliferous. As with most fabric items, collector interest is low. Values are 1 - 25 depending on age and interest
of item … 30's items slightly higher.

S3275   S3291

S3280   S3295

S3310

S3340

S3360

S3400

S3635

S3400

S3400

S3590

S3575

Many Selling Features

have created an enormous demand for this silverplate featuring

DISNEY CHARACTER PATTERNS

To the beauty and utility of this line we add many special selling features. Toys, hand-painted wooden cut-outs, bibs, special gift boxes and display material enable any department to attract wide-spread public interest.

These features plus the faithful reproductions of the world's favorite characters on each piece of merchandise are making it difficult for us to keep pace with the demand.

Write for full particulars

INTERNATIONAL SILVER CO.

Division of

Meriden, Conn.

DIVISION OFFICES

New York · Chicago · St. Louis
9-15 Maiden Lane · Merchandise Mart · Ambassador Bldg.
San Francisco—130 First Street

S3511   S3577   S3576   S3578   S3510

Licensed manufacturers — Babcock Phillips division of Dart Industries (Richmond, VA) 1974-80, pillows; Bates Mfg. Co. (Lewiston, ME) 1955-56, cotton bedspreads and draperies; The Bibb Co. (NYC) 1982-84, bedspreads, pillows, etc.; Calorama, Inc. (LA) 1947-48, chenille bedspreads; Crawford Furniture Mfg. Co. (St. Charles, IL) 1934-35, pillows; Judy Crib Sheet Co. (Long Beach, CA) 1953, crib sheets, juvenile sheets and pillow cases; A. P. McAuley Co. (NYC) 1950-55, bedspreads; Pacific Chenille Craft Co. (LA) 1940-41 bedspreads; Palmer Brothers Co. (NYC) 1933-34, comforts and bedspreads; Peirce & Cutler, Inc. (LA) 1948, 49, chenille bedspreads; Perfect Fit Industries, Inc. (NYC) 1968, bedspreads and blankets; Philip Labe (NYC) 1935-37, pillow tops, table covers, etc.; R & M Industries (San Marcos, CA) 1980-82, decorator pillows; L. S. Sutton & Sons, Inc. (NYC) 1973, novelty decorated pillows; and Wamsutta Mills, Inc. (NYC) 1968-84, sheets, pillow cases, bedspreads and other textile products.

S3500 SILVER CUPS, PLATES, BOWLS, SILVERWARE AND FLATWARE

Silver products were popular baby gifts in the 30's. Mickey Mouse, Snow White and Pinocchio silverware was available from 1931-42 and in 1947-48. The Wm. Rogers spoon offered by *Post-O* cereal is one of the most common. Davy Crockett and Mickey Mouse Club cutlery sets were produced in the 50's. Mary Poppins pieces were made in the 60's and Disney main character flatware was introduced and has remained available 1970 to present. The 1931 William Rogers & Son (later International Silver Co.) eating utensils were sold with the Borgfeldt lollypop hands wooden Mickey Mouse figure. By 1934 the company was still using some Borgfeldt pieces (such as small wood Mickey in row boat), but had begun to create a special line of pull toys (perhaps made for them by N. N. Hill Brass Co.). Sets were also gift boxed for older children. Oneida and Silvercraft of California were other 40's makers. All pieces are silverplate.

1847 Rogers Bros. (William Rogers & Son, succeeded (by International Silver Co. S3505-S3599)

S3505	Borgfeldt doll with spoon and fork	500 - 1800
S3510	Mickey row boat with cup	400 - 1500
S3511	Three Pigs items on wooden cut-outs, each	60 - 150
S3512	Cup or eating utensils on pull toy	80 - 800
S3540	Character silver sets, boxed	60 - 500
S3550	Mickey or Minnie, baby spoon or fork, cereal spoon, child's knife, fork or spoon, each	4 - 12
S3575	Three Pigs baby spoon or fork, each	5 - 15
S3576	Three Pigs youth knife, fork or spoon, each	5 - 15
S3577	Mickey napkin rings, each	10 - 40
S3578	Mickey or other character, silver cup	20 - 80
S3580	Silver porringer, cereal bowl or baby plate, each	25 - 75
S3590	Snow White baby spoon or fork, each	5 - 14
S3591	Snow White child's knife, fork or spoon, each	4 - 12
S3599	Pinocchio, child's knife, fork or spoon, each	5 - 15
S3600	Snow White silver cup (Cartier)	25 - 100
S3610	Silvercraft of California sets	25 - 150
S3611	Cup (SOC)	15 - 75
S3612	Fork, spoon or baby spoon (SOC), each	4 - 12
S3613	Napkin ring (SOC)	5 - 25
S3625	Disneyland souvenir sugar spoon ©1954	8 - 32
S3630	Davy Crockett fork or spoon, flatware, each	3 - 8
S3635	Mickey Mouse Club cutlery set (Plastic Metal)	8 - 22
S3636	Individual pieces from S3635, each	2 - 5
S3650	Mary Poppins sugar spoon (1964) International Silver	4 - 12

S3580

S3550

S3540

S3505

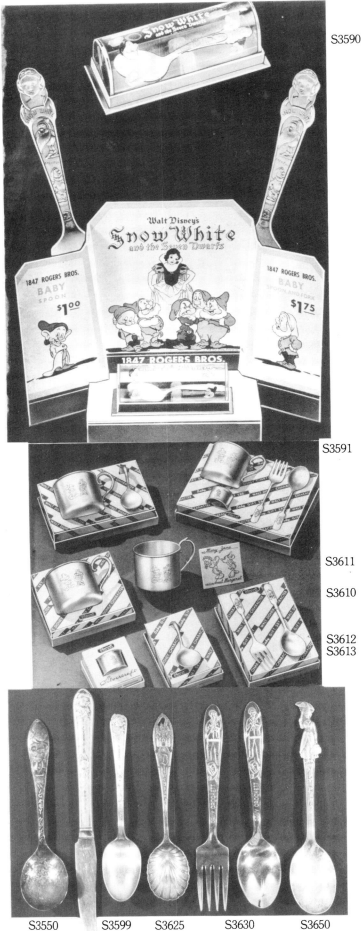

S3590

S3591

S3611

S3610

S3612
S3613

S3550   S3599   S3625   S3630   S3650

Licensed manufacturers — America Metalcrafts Co. (Attleboro, MA) 1947-48; Bonny Products, Inc. (Lynnbrook, NY) 1970-84, children's flatware and ice cream scoopers; Fort, Inc. (E. Providence, RI) 1980-84, character collectible spoons (silverplate and pewter); International Silver Co. successor to William Rogers and Son (Meriden, CT) 1931-74, silverware, cups, bowls, collector's plates and medals; Oneida Ltd. (Oneida, NY) 1940-42, silverware; Plastic Metal Mfg. Co. (Chicago) 1957-62; William Rogers and Son (see International Silver Co.); and Wallace Silversmiths (Wallingford, CT) 1972, silver and silver plated spoons, cups and porringer sets.

S3512

S3512

S4000 SKATES

Reportedly there were some Mickey Mouse roller skates from the 30's, but research did not uncover the product or licensee. Globe-Union Inc. (Milwaukee, WI) made roller skates (1957-59), plus American Lighting Specialties (Torrance, CA) made ice and roller skates (1981-83). Value range for identified licensees is 2 - 15.

S4200 SLEDS

S. L. Allen & Co., Inc. (Philadelphia, PA) made character sleds (1935-40) in two sizes. Mickey and Minnie, Donald and Nephews, and Snow White and the 7 Dwarfs were the three different decal designs on each of the two sizes. Value 45 - 150

S5000 SOAP AND BUBBLE BATH

Figural soap of Borgfeldt import was advertised in the Dec 1931 *Good Housekeeping* magazine. It was made by D. H. & Co. of London, England. There were two other soap licensees beginning in 1932, but the figural products of the Lightfoot Schultz Co. (1934-42) are the best known to collectors. The colorful boxes are also prized. Bar soap with transfer pictures was made by Pictorial Products, Inc. in 1934. Monogram added shampoo to bar soap sets in the 40's. Colgate-Palmolive-Peet Co. introduced Soaky soap bars in the 50's and liquid Soaky bubble bath in figural plastic containers around 1968.

S5003 Mickey or Minnie, figural (D. H. & Co.), each   50 - 150
S5015 Mickey Mouse toilet soap (Pictorial Products)   20 - 60

S5015

S5020

S4000

S4200

S4200

S5003

FERDINAND

S5060

S5061

97

S5045

S5030

S5052   S5063

1936 Lightfoot Schultz ad.

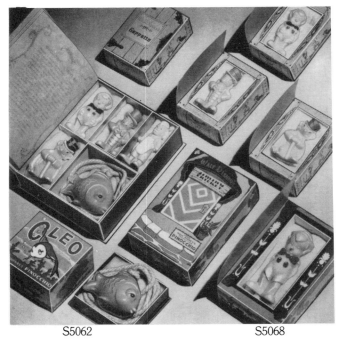

S5062   S5068

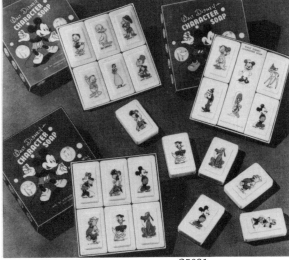

S5091

98

Lightfoot Schultz Co. (S5020-S5070)

S5020	Boxed sets, Mickey, Donald, Pluto or Elmer Elephant in various combinations, each multi-character box	30 - 150
S5030	Same characters as S5020, individually boxed	20 - 70
S5031	Same as 5020, individual unboxed soap, each	8 - 35
S5045	Snow White and 7 Dwarfs set in book box	45 - 85
S5052	Individual boxed soaps from S5045, each	7 - 20
S5053	Individual unboxed soaps from S5045	4 - 9
S5054	Same soap as in 5045, only 1968 reissue in clear plastic top package instead of book	18 - 45
S5060	Ferdinand the Bull (2 versions) boxed	8 - 18
S5061	Same as 5060, unboxed	2 - 12
S5062	Pinocchio book boxed set — Pinocchio, Jiminy Cricket, Geppetto, Honest John, and Cleo (on rope) set	50 - 100
S5063	Same as S5062 in individual boxes, each	10 - 50
S5068	Large size Pinocchio or Jiminy Cricket, boxed	12 - 60
S5075	Same as S5062 or S5068, without boxes	5 - 18
S5080	Molded full figure (Kerk Guild) each	4 - 15
S5081	Same as S5080, boxed set, Donald, Mickey and Pluto	15 - 50
S5082	Bath ball, Donald, Mickey or Pluto, head only (Kerk Guild), each	6 - 20
S5090	Monogram character soap sets, 2 to 6 bars with or without shampoo, each set	8 - 35
S5091	Individual bars or bottles from S5090, each	1 - 4
S5094	Alice in Wonderland soap collection	20 - 60
S6020	Soaky soap bar dispenser, picture and bars,	8 - 40
S6021	Character wrapper bars (6 different), each	1 - 3
S6030	Soaky figural bottles, Snow White, Dopey, Mickey, Donald, Bambi and others, each	2 - 6
S6045	Avon Mickey or Pluto, each	2 - 15
S6050	Theme park souvenir soap sets	3 - 10

Licensed manufacturers — Avon Products, Inc. (NYC) 1970-71, soaps, bubble bath and shampoo; Colgate-Palmolive-Peet Co. (NYC) 1937-40, 1953 (Peter Pan Soap), 50's Soaky bar soap, 1968 began Soaky liquid bubble bath; Hawthorne House, Inc. (Bloomington, IL) 1972-73, soap making set; Walter J. Jamieson Corp. (NYC) 1955-59, Lady and the Tramp children's bath sets and Mickey molded soap; Kerk Guild, Inc. (NYC) 1949-57, figural soaps; Lehn & Fink Products Corp. (Bloomfield, NJ) 1958, bubble bath; Lightfoot Schultz Co. (NYC) 1934-42; Manhattan Soap Co. (Hollywood, CA) 1942-53, decorated soaps and liquid bubble bath; Parfait, Inc. (Chicago, IL) 1950-52, sachets, molded soap figures and bath salts; Pictorial Products Co. (NYC) 1934, toilet soap with transfer pictures; Irvine W. Rice (NYC) 1931-32, importer of D. H. & Co. (D. Harris & Co.) figural soaps; Ben Rickert, Inc. (Wayne, NJ) 1980-84; Stephen Riley Co. (LA) 1952-59, bubble bath; Superior Toy and Mfg. Co., Inc. (Chicago) 1981-84, fun showers; and Tre-Jur (NYC) 1968, dusting powder, cologne and molded soaps.

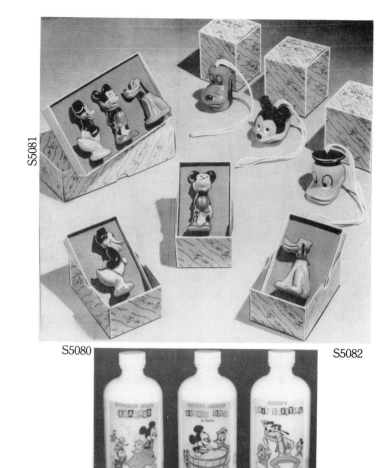

S5081

S5080   S5082

S6050

S5090

S6021   S6020

S6030

S5205

S5600

S5500

S5200 SPARKLERS

One toy in Borgfleldt's 1932 ad is a mechanical sparkler. Another was done for the Bicentennial in 1976.(See Wind-Up Toys for Mickey/Felix sparkler.)

S5205 Mickey's head	50 - 150
S5250 Minuteman Mickey (Chein)	4 - 12

Licensed manufacturers — George Borgfeldt & Co. (NYC) 1931-41; and Chein Playthings (Burlington, NJ) 1976.

S5500 SPONGE TOYS

Virginia Hall made rubber bath sponges in 1953 and a number of other companies have followed with products along the same line. James Industries made Snow White character compressed sponge toys in 1968 and Poly Soft made foam puzzles and blocks. As with most rubber products, there is no way to preserve these destined-to-crumble artifacts. Thus they have little value.
Licensed manufacturers — Amsco Corp. (NYC) 1968, sponge bath toys; Virginia Hall, Inc. (Macon, GA) 1953-54, rubber bath sponges; James Industries, Inc. (Hollidaysburg, PA) 1968, compressed sponge toys; and Poly Soft Products Corp. unit of Sponge Specialties Corp. (E. Rockaway, NJ) 1972-84, polyurethane foam block and jigsaw puzzles, story block, bowling set, play pads, sponges, bath mats and mitts.

S5600 SPORTING GOODS

Draper-Maynard made a full line of Mickey Mouse sporting goods in 1933. A. L. S. Industries made sports toys and accessories in 1984. In between were a number of sleeping bag and frisbee producers.

S5610 Mickey Mouse bat, baseball, baseball gloves, boxing gloves, football or basketball (Draper-Maynard), each	10 - 60
S5625 Sleeping bags, each	3 - 15
S5650 Frisbees, each	2 - 14

Licensed manufacturers — A. L. S. (American Lighting Specialties) Industries, Inc. (Torrance, CA) 1984, children's sport toys and accessories; Draper-Maynard Co. (NYC) 1933-34; Ero Industries (Chicago) 1982-84, slumber bags; Homemaker Industries division of Beatrice Foods Co. (Chicago), then Sportsline (Shawnee Mission, KS) 1976-81, sleeping bags; S & R Infants Wear Co., Inc. (NYC) 1958-59, sleeping bags; Skyway Products, Inc. (Brooklyn, NY) 1972-73, frisbees; and Walt Disney Distributing Co. (Lake Buena Vista, FL) 1971-77, punching bags.

S6000 STAMPS — POSTAGE

Following Walt Disney's death in 1966, a U. S. commemrative postage stamp was issued in his honor. Disney artist Bob Moore designed the stamp, but since the stamp could not be copyrighted, no regular Disney characters could be used. The interest in the Disney stamp worldwide prompted Inter-Government Philatelic Corp. (NYC) to seek a license to make it possible for foreign countries to issue stamps depicting Disney characters. Through their efforts character stamps and special sheets are issued on a regular basis in a growing number of countries including Anguilla, Antigua, Bhuntan, Dominica, Gambia, Greneda, Greneda Grenadines, Republic of Maldives, Redonda, Saint Lucia and the Turks

S5610

S6000

and Caicos Islands. For Disneyana purposes, each set has a special album and often a companion souvenir sheet. Most packages are designed to sell "new" for 10 - 12. Prior to the success of these offerings there were some infringing sets from Persian Gulf sheikdoms. The resale market is estimated by the regular postage stamp collector price catalogs. A 1984 stamp journal ad offers 305 different for $49.95. The stamps are promoted similar to Franklin Mint silver medalions. Samples of these stamps are interesting. Real values are unlikely to increase much beyond the offering price so long as there are new issues available.

S6200 STAMPS — POSTER

Stamp collecting became a national hobby in the great Depression 30's. An offshoot of the mushrooming mania for stamps was the National Poster Stamp Society (Chicago), a private organization that authorized and promoted private issues of collector stamps. Today, most of the issues they sponsored are worthless. There were, however, two Disney promotional issues. A set of 8 Snow White stamps offered by Armour & Co. (Certificate No. 47) and a 32 stamp Pinocchio series (Certificate No. 88) used as a traffic builder promotion by IGA — The Independent Grocers' Alliance. The IGA stamps were issued four to a sealed envelope, and an attractive album for the complete collection was given free in store or 5¢ by mail.

S6251	Sheet of 8 Snow White poster stamps	10 - 30
S6252	Individual poster stamps from S6251, each	1 - 2
S6255	Pinocchio IGA poster stamp album	10 - 50
S6256	Album complete with all 32 stamps	50 - 175
S6257	Pinocchio IGA envelope with 4 stamps	2 - 10
S6258	Individual stamps for S6355, each	1 - 3

S6500 STATIONERY AND NOTE PAPER

This class includes boxed or padded stationery or note paper. (For Walt Disney Productions letterhead, see L4000.) Davis & Holly are the first licensee on record, quickly followed by Powers Paper. Kemper-Thomas, Hobby Stationers and Whitman did attractive sets in the 40's.

S6520	Mickey Mouse Stationery pad (Powers)	15 - 50
S6538	Peter and the Wolf (Hobby)	8 - 20
S6540	Donald Duck Writing Paper (Whitman)	5 - 15
S6550	Alice in Wonderland stationery set (Whitman)	8 - 25
S6558	Mickey Mouse Club Note Paper	5 - 15
S6580	Mickey Mouse Club Stationery (1977)	3 - 8
S6590	Theme park souvenir stationery	3 - 8

Licensed manufacturers — Davis & Holly, Inc. (NYC) 1932; Hobby Stationers (Kansas City, MO) 1945-45; I. S. I. Special Graphics Products, Inc. (Hicksville, NY) 1983, rub-down notecard, stationery and postcard kit; Kemper-Thomas Co. (Cincinnati, OH) 1943-44; Stationers Specialty Corp. (NYC) 1938-39; Tara Toy Co. (Glendale, NY) 1981-82, miniature toy desk accessories and organizers; and Whitman Publishing Co. (Racine, WI) 1933-85.

S7000 STICKERS AND STICKER BOOKS

Collins-Kirk, Inc. made "Sticker Tots" paper cut-outs in 1932. There were Mickey "surprise stickers" for the bottoms of milk glasses about the same time. If you drank all your milk, you saw one of Mickey's pals on the bottom of your empty glass. There have been cut-out stickers over the years and many used for Walt Disney Productions promotional use. Hallmark, Ambassador and Drawing Board have produced lines of decorative stickers. The British have produced Disney promotional stickers and Panini of Italy has done a series of stickers and sticker books in English, French, German and Italian. Only the Americana series album was sold in the U. S., but all but the German series were sold in Canada.

S7008	Mickey Mouse Surprise Stickers and health chart	50 - 150
S7015	Trimz Kut-Outs, Mickey or Donald, each	5 - 15
S7020	Mickey Mouse Club stickers, each	1 - 3
S7024	WDP promotional stickers	1 - 5
S7030	Decorative stickers, per package	1 - 4
S7040	Panini sticker sets and albums, Mickey Mouse and His Friends (1977), Disneyland (Benjamin Bilder), Mickey Story (1978), Elliott Pete's Dragon (1978), The Rescuers Bernard and Bianca (1978), Bambi (1979), The Black	

S6257   S6258   S6255

S6251

S6558

S6538   S6550

S6580

S7015   S6540   S7008

Canadian sticker set. Value 18 - 50.

S7024   S7020

S7030

S7040   S7040

Hole (1979) or Goofy Olympique (1980), each set
and album   15 - 35
Licensed manufacturers — Collins-Kirk, Inc. (Chicago) 1932; Ever Ready
Label Corp. (NYC) 1955-56, Mickey Mouse Club stickers; Hallmark
Cards, Inc. (Kansas City, MO) 1972-84; Edizioni Panini S. P. A. (Modena,
Italy) 1977-80; and Trimz Co., Inc. (Chicago) 1947-48.

S8500 STOVES

The Metal Ware Corp. (Two Rivers, WI) 1936-37 made Mickey
Mouse stoves in two models. The regular toy store original sold for
50¢. The electrified version retailed for a dollar. Current values are
35 - 150.

Also see — COOKWARE AND KITCHEN SETS

S9000 STRAWS AND PUMPS

The Herz Mfg. Corp. made Disney paper drinking straws from
1948-55, but they were available in stores until the late 60's and
there were still plenty salted away in old warehouses to await a
boom in Disneyana. They are nice and colorful, but not rare.
Morris Plastics made a milk pump in the early 50's. Mickey Mouse
Club character "See-Straws" were produced until 1958.

S9010	Mickey or Donald Sunshine Straws (Herz)	3 - 6
S9011	Donald super long straws (Herz)	4 - 8
S9012	Individual wrapped straws, each	1 - 2
S9020	Mickey or Donald "SEE-STRAW" (Jolly)	3 - 10

Licensed manufacturers — General Foods (Jello Division) 1958, Jiminy
Cricket straws; Herz Mfg. Corp. (NYC) 1948-55; Jolly Blinker Co., Inc.
(NYC) 1955-58; Maryland Paper Products Co., Inc. division of Maryland
Cup Corp. (Owings Mills, MD) 1968, paper drinking straws; Morris Plas-
tics Corp. (NYC) c. 1952-54; and Weclite Co., Inc. (Teaneck, NJ) 1982-84,
straight and flex plastic drinking straws.

S8500

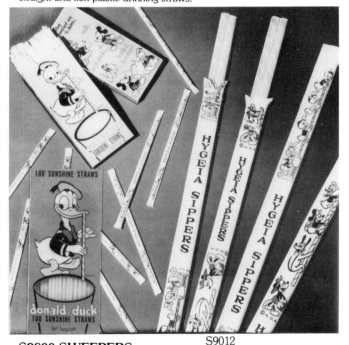

S9012

S9800 SWEEPERS

A Mickey litho tin box sweeper was first made by Ohio Art Co.
(Bryan, OH) in 1936. Donald and Dopey versions quickly followed. No sweepers were listed in Ohio Arts 1940 ads. A Cinderella version was made in England by Wells-Brimtoy Distributions,
Ltd.

S9804	Mickey Mouse sweeper (1936)	20 - 110
S9805	Donald sweeper (1937)	15 - 85
S9806	Dopey sweeper (1938)	15 - 55
S9820	Cinderella sweeper (1950)	15 - 45

S9900 SWIMMING POOLS AND ACCESSORIES

Inflatable swimming pools were made since the 40's by the
manufacturers listed at I5000. Those listed here are solid vacuum-
formed pools made by the Muskin Corp. (Wilkes-Barre, PA)
1976-79. Value 5 - 10. Older inflatable designs are valued at 5 -15.
Inflatable and foam pool accessories are equally unexciting to

Milk pump. Value 4 - 15.

S9011   S9020   S9010

S9806

S9804

S9820

CHILDREN'S DISHES—handle mugs, cereal bowls, plates and feeding dishes—in green, red, yellow—all with two-color reproductions of Mickey Mouse and other Disney characters—all to retail profitably at 15c each! Breakfast sets, attractively boxed at 50c retail! Tea party sets in green, yellow, red, pink and blue—with Walt Disney designs in 2 colors—assembled in stunning gift boxes! Each and every item illustrated is a big volume number!

Write for full particulars

Hemco Molding Division

THE BRYANT ELECTRIC COMPANY
Licensee
Bridgeport, Connecticut

T2020

T2035   T2036

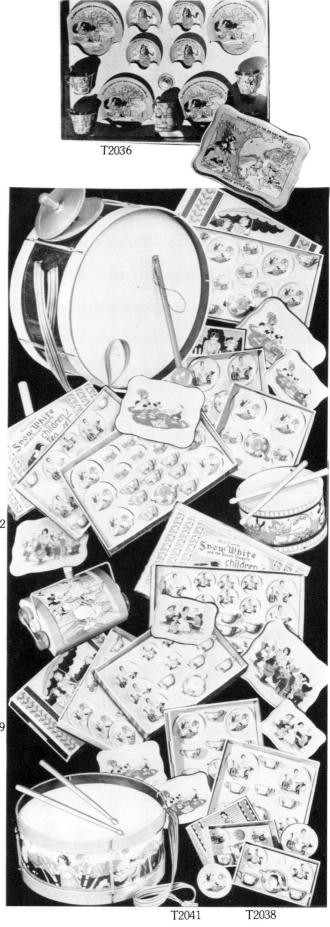

T2036

T2042

T2039

T2041   T2038

104

collectors with values ranging 3 - 12. One pool accessories manufacturer not listed at INFLATABLES is Utility Chemical Co. (Patterson, NJ) 1984.

T0200 TABLE LINENS AND NAPKINS

Tablecloths and napkins were made by many textile licensees listed at S3400 and other makers. The Smith, Hogg & Co., Inc. (NYC) 1935-37 made the most collectible products in this class. Valued at 10 - 60. Sponge Clean Products (NYC) 1972-73 and Sterling Novelty Products Co. (Chicago) 1975 (coloring tablecloths) are more recent producers. Valued at 3 - 10 each.

T1500 TATTOOS AND TRANSFERS

B. Gordon Press made Mickey Mouse "Tat-ooh!" that sold by the 1¢ sheet or 10¢ book (1944-46). Cockamamies skin pictures were marketed by Dynamic Toy Inc. in 1961. Donald Duck transfers from Tower Press (London) and Disney Tattoos by Dandy (Denmark) were somehow sold in the U. S.

T1505	Mickey Tat-ooh! display	20 - 50
T1506	Mickey book of 120 Tat-ooh! pictures	10 - 25
T1510	Donald Duck transfers display	10 - 35
T1520	Wonderful World of Color or Pinocchio Cockamamies	5 - 15

Licensed manufacturers — Dandy Factories (Vejle, Denmark) c. 1980; Dynamic Toy Inc. (NYC) 1961; and B. Gordon Press (NYC) 1944-46.

Also see EASTER EGG DYE & TRANSFER SETS and RUB-ON TRANSFERS).

T2000 TEA SETS

The first children's tea sets were china. (see CHINAWARE C6100). Ohio Art introduced litho tin sets in 1933. Beetleware (one of the first plastics) sets came along in 1934. Larger tea sets contained enough place setting for six or eight children (or dolls). Small metal sets included a tea pot, cream, sugar, cups and saucers and serving tray. Large metal sets include extra place settings plus dinner plates and a larger tray. T2020 Beetleware tea party sets with 3, 4 or 6 place settings (1934-37), values on all tea sets depend on size, completeness and if set is in original box. 20 - 125

Ohio Art Company (T2030-T2045)

T2030	Mickey/Minnie tea set for 2	20 - 60
T2031	Mickey/Minnie tea set for 6	45 - 120
T2035	3 Pigs tea set for 2 or 3	25 - 70
T2036	3 Pigs tea set for 4 or 6	50 - 150
T2038	Snow White tea set for 2 or 3	15 - 45
T2039	Snow White tea set for 4 or 6	25 - 80
T2041	Donald/Clara picnic tea set for 2 or 3	15 - 45
T2042	Donald/Clara picnic tea set for 4 or 6	25 - 80
T2044	Pinocchio tea set for 2	25 - 75
T2045	Pinocchio tea set for 6	75 - 160
T2060	Mickey/Minnie/Donald/Pluto tea set (Chein) 1952	20 - 50
T2070	Snow White plastic pot and cups (Chein) 1968	10 - 35
T2075	Mickey/Goofy/Pluto with plastic pot and cups	8 - 25
T2080	Worcester illustrated plastic sets, each	5 - 22
T2090	Alice In Wonderland (china) theme park souvenir ('80's)	3 - 6
T2150	Litho tin English sets sold in Canada, each	15 - 60

Licensed manufacturers — The Bryant Electric Co. (Bridgeport, CT) 1934-37; J. Chein & Co. (NYC) 1953-55, 68; Ohio Art Co. (Bryan, OH) 1933-42, 44-45, 82; and Worcester Toy Co. division of Plascor, Inc. (Worcester, MA) 1972-79.

T1510

T1505

T1506

T1520

T2031

T2044

T2045

T2020

T2020

T2150

J. CHEIN & CO.

"Snow White Tea Sets" #209

A Fairy Tale tea set with Snow White and her cute seven little dwarfs. Set consists of 3 cups . . . 3 saucers . . . 3 regular size plates and a large 5"x7" serving tray. Suggested retail price $1.29

"Big Value Tea Set" #230

Includes 3 large cups . . . 3 large plates . . . 3 regular plates . . . plastic tea pot and large serving tray. Suggested retail price $2.49

J. Chein & Co., Williams St., Burlington, N. J. or 200 Fifth Ave., N. Y. 10010 (Contact Morris Dorfman)

T2070

T4092   T4093   T4094

T3550

T4005

T3520   T3530   T3540   T3575

T2500 TELEPHONES

The majority of children's telephones of collector interest were made by N. N. Hill Brass Co. and will be found illustrated at the PULL TOY classification (P7800). Hasbro made an early talking telephone in 1964. American Telecommunications Corp. was licensed to produce Mickey Mouse and Winnie the Pooh figural telephones for most of the major phone companies in the U. S.

T2512	Mickey Mouse cradle telephone (1933)	20 - 80
T2513	Mickey coin telephone with 1¢, 5¢ and 10¢ slots (1936)	25 - 85
T2516	Mickey or Donald upright phone, each	15 - 45
T2525	Snow White and Dopey cradle phone	20 - 50
T2526	Doc upright phone	20 - 50
T2530	Mickey and Donald cradle phone	25 - 55
T2540	Mickey talking (pay) telephone (Hasbro)	8 - 30
T2580	Mickey operating phone, rotary dial or touch tone	50 - 120
T2581	Winnie the Pooh operating phone, either style	55 - 125

Licensed manufacturers — American Telephone Corp. (El Monte, CA) 1976-84; Hasbro-Hassenfeld Brothers, Inc. (Pawtucket, RI) talking telephone, 1969; and the N. N. Hill Brass Company (East Hampton, CT) 1933-42.

T3000 THERMOMETERS

There was a litho tin Mickey thermometer made by Character Art Mfg. Co. (Brooklyn, NY) 1935-37 (value 25 - 100 and Plastic Novelties, Inc. (NYC) Jiminy Cricket and Pinocchio versions in 1940-41 valued at 20 - 50 each. Thermometers are attached to various other products, some associated with calendar manufacturers.

Also see — CALENDARS, PENCIL SHARPENERS and TILES

T3500 TILES

Ceramic tiles made by the Kemper-Thomas Co. (Cincinnati, OH) 1943-44 were sold in stores (20¢ each) as small wall plaques. They were also used as specialty advertising premiums. There were two sizes — 4-1/4" square and 6" square. Round tiles featuring Donald and Scrooge are more recent, but have no marks to indicate the source. See AMERICA ON PARADE for logo tile.

T3520	Kemper-Thomas 6" character plaque, Mickey, Donald, Pluto, Goofy, Bambi or Thumper, each	3 - 15
T3530	Kemper-Thomas 6" thermometer plaque series, Mickey, Donald, Pluto, Goofy, Lullaby Land, Ugly Duckling, Three Little Kittens or Water Babies, each	4 - 20
T3540	Kemper-Thomas "Sportsman" series, with thermometers, golfing, bowling, fishing and baseball, each	4 - 20
T3550	Kemper-Thomas 4-1/4" advertising plaques, each	5 - 20
T3575	Donald or Scrooge round plaques, each	6 - 22

T4000 TIN BOXES AND CONTAINERS

Tin containers, mainly for candy, have been made since 1930. England has been the largest producer, but many others were made throughout Europe well into the 40's. There was a resurgence in tin candy boxes in the late 70's. Hallmark also used one to package a Bambi puzzle.

T4005	Early Mickey candy tins, 30's and 40's	30 - 100
T4020	Snow White chocolate candy box	50 - 120
T4080	Bambi's puzzle box (Hallmark)	2 - 10
T4082	New Mickey Mouse Club tin (Hallmark)	2 - 8
T4090	Round Snow White candy tin	2 - 8
T4092	American Candy, Collector's Edition Volume 1	2 - 10
T4093	American Candy, Collector's Edition Volume 2	2 - 8
T4094	American Candy, Collector's Edition Volume 3 or 4	2 - 7
T4098	Mickey's Christmas Carol	2 - 7
T4100	Bank candy tins, Pinocchio, Sleeping Beauty, Mickey and characters (blue), or Donald and characters (orange), sold at theme park candy shops (Kinnerton), each	2 - 5
T4120	Strawberry Fantasy bath powder bank tin (Rickert)	1 - 4

Licensed manufacturers — American Candy Mfg. Co. (Selma, AL) 1976-84; George Borgfeldt & Co. (NYC) 1931-41; Hallmark Cards, Inc. (Kansas City, MO) 1972-84; Kinnerton (Long Island City, NY) 1983-85 but pre-

T2512   T2530

T3000

T2540

T3000

T4005

T4020

T5002

T4100

T4090   T4082   T4080

SPRING OF 1983 OPENING

POST CARDS

1st Anniversary
Tokyo Disneyland.

T5002

Tokyo Disneyland
The Happiest Place on Earth

T5024

JAPAN AIR LINES

T5015 T5014

T5026

GRAND OPENING
APRIL 15, 1983

SPRING OF 1983 OPENING!
Tokyo Disneyland.

The Small World Days
Tokyo Disneyland.

Tokyo Disneyland.
HAPPY BIRTHDAY
DONALD DUCK

Tokyo Disneyland.

Tokyo Disneyland.
2nd ANNIVERSARY
APRIL 15, 1985

T5027

Entertainment
SHOW INFORMATION
ライブ・エンターテイメント
ご案内

T5022

GRAND OPENING
April 15, 1983

T5016

Tokyo Disneyland.   Tokyo Disneyland.

T5025

Tokyo Disneyland.   Tokyo Disneyland.

T5030

108

viously a supplier from London; and Ben Richert Inc. (Wayne, NJ) 1980-84.

T5000 TOKYO DISNEYLAND

Tokyo Disneyland officially opened April 15, 1983 following many years of preparation and negotiations leading to a joint venture agreement signed between the Oriental Land Co. (composed mainly of Mitsui Real Estate Development Co. and Keisei Electric Railway Co.) and Walt Disney Productions. The announced construction cost was $400 million, exclusive of land created by landfill in Tokyo Bay. The Magic Kingdom consists of five themed lands — World Bazaar (fully climatized replacement for Main Street U.S.A.), Adventureland, Westernland, Fantasyland and Tomorrowland surrounding Cinderella Castle. Missing is the train station and Town Square. The train circles Adventureland and Westernland only. The Mickey Mouse Revue from Walt Disney World was moved to Tokyo to join new units of the most popular attractions from the U. S. parks. Disney promotion and merchandising know-how was part of the package so Tokyo Disneyland has been an abundant source of Disneyana. The value of this material is supported largely by its remote accessability. The demand for material, however, has resulted in a good system by which Tokyo Disneyland items may be obtained by mail. The address is: Tokyo Disneyland Mail Order Service c/o Merchandise Division 1-1, Maihama, Urayasu-shi, Chiba-ken, 270-01 Japan. Already the amount of material created by the park is beyond the scope of this book. The items listed are mainly pre-opening, opening day and first year of operation Disneyana.

T5001

T5000

T5001	Pre-opening announcement folder	5 - 10
T5002	Folder of pre-opening postcards, 2 sets, each	8 - 18
T5014	Employee opening day button	18 - 37
T5015	Opening day button, souvenir	20 - 35
T5016	Opening day employee medallion and folder	15 - 30
T5020	Opening day medallion, 3", metal or silver	30 - 70
T5022	Pocket guidebooks in English, Japanese or Chinese, each	1 - 4
T5023	Guide map	2 - 10
T5024	Souvenir booklet	2 - 8
T5025	Character souvenir buttons, each	3 - 9
T5026	Special promotion buttons, each	5 - 20
T5027	Anniversary, Christmas, Donald or Mickey birthday buttons, each	4 - 15
T5030	Patches or decals, each	1 - 5

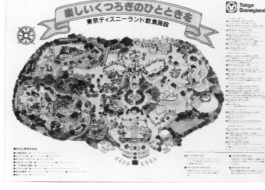

T5023

The list is ever growing, but many dealers are getting into the business of importing the most collectible items so Tokyo Disneyland may become familiar even though a visit may never be possible.

T6000 TOOL BOXES AND SETS

Hamilton Metal Products Co. (Hamilton, OH) 1935-36 made five different tool chest designs in three different sizes. These are found with some regularity, but seldom with the toy tools. Value range 20 - 100. American Toy & Furniture Co., Inc. (Chicago) 1956-57 produced Mickey Mouse Club tool chest sets valued at 15 - 35.

T6100 TOOTHBRUSHES AND TOOTHPASTE

Hughes made toothbrushes from 1934-41 while Nevins Drug Co. supplied Mickey toothpaste. Lever Brothers has been marketing modern day toothbrushes since 1970. Kenner Products made an electric version in 1972 and Helms Toy Corp. added a 30's looking talking version in 1979.

T6105	Figural Mickey on handle (1934)	25 - 100
T6108	Hughes Mickey with decal on handle	15 - 55
T6110	Nevins Drug Co. Mickey toothpaste tube	30 - 120

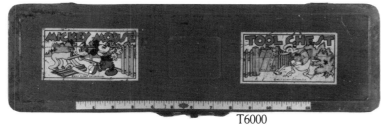

T6000

T6000

T6000

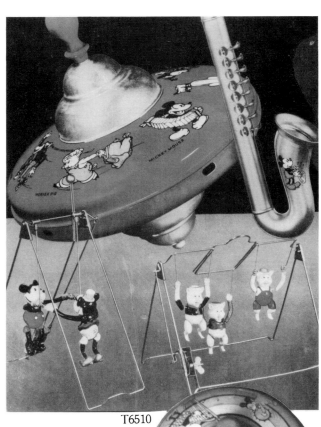

T6510

T6510

MICKEY MOUSE SHEETS AND TOWELS

ALSO WASH CLOTHS
BIBS, PILLOWCASES, SPREADS AND BLANKETS

TOWELS, WASH CLOTHS, BIBS   CANDLEWICK SPREADS
Manufactured by   Manufactured by
MARTEX DIVISION   I. T. BATES CANDLEWICKS
Wellington Sears Co., New York   Dalton, Georgia

SHEETS, PILLOWCASES, CRIB BLANKETS
Manufactured by
NASHUA MFG COMPANY
Nashua, New Hampshire

Sold and distributed exclusively by

SMITH, HOGG & CO., INC.
Licensee

99 Chauncy St.   115-117 Worth St.   323 S. Franklin St.
Boston   New York   Chicago

T6800

T6800

T6910

T6115 Snow White/Seven Dwarf toothbrushes, each	12 - 45
T6118 Pinocchio toothbrush (Hughes)	15 - 50
T6140 Lever Brothers Toothbrushes	1 - 2

Licensed manufacturers — Helm Toy Corp. (NYC) 1979-84; Henry L. Hughes Co. Inc. and successor Hughes-Autograf Brush Co., Inc. (NYC) 1934-41; Kenner Products Co. (Cincinnati, OH) 1972-74; Lever Brothers Co., Inc. (NYC) 1970-84; Nevins Drug Co. (Philadelphia, PA) 1935-37; and The Pepsodent Co. (NYC) 1938-39, sold regular toothpaste and related products using Disney ads, premiums and promotions.

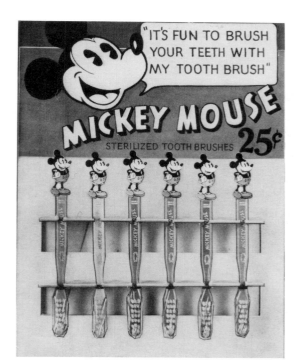

T6400 TOOTHBRUSH HOLDERS

George Borgfeldt & Co. (NYC) 1931-41 was the importer of Japanese porcelain bisque toothbrush holders. There were single figure Mickey or Minnie figural designs for a single toothbrush and various characters or group designs to accommodate multiple toothbrushes. (See FIGURES — PORCELAIN BISQUE for individual figural listing). Miller Studios, Inc. (New Philadelphia, OH) 1975-76 also produced toothbrush holders.

T6405 Mickey with hanky to Pluto's nose	50 - 120
T6406 Mickey and Minnie on couch, Pluto at feet	45 - 90
T6407 Mickey and Minnie standing	40 - 80
T6410 Three Pigs, Practical laying bricks	35 - 70
T6411 Three Pigs at brick piano	40 - 75
T6414 Long bill Donald at water fountain (or pillar)	80 - 450
T6415 Long bill Donald, profile	60 - 300
T6416 Twin long bill Donalds	55 - 175
T6418 Donald, arms around Mickey and Minnie	50 - 120
T6420 Dumbo	70 - 200

T6500 TOPS

George Borgfeldt & Co. sold tin little musical tops made by Fritz Bueschel circa 1933-39. These came in several different sizes ranging from 6-1/2" to 14" in diameter. Chein made similar tops periodically in the 50's and 60's and from 1972-84. Kidco, Inc. made unique figural tops (1981-82)

T6108

T6510 Bueschel spinning toys, various sizes, each	20 - 120
T6530 Chein musical tops, various sizes (50's), each	15 - 45
T6535 Chein musical tops, various sizes (1968-84)	5 - 25
T6560 Kidco figural tops, Mickey, Donald, Goofy or Pluto, each	4 - 15

Licensed manufacturers — Fritz Bueschel via Borgfeldt (Hackettstown, NJ) c. 1933-39; J. Chein & Co., Inc. (Newark, NJ) 1953-55, 68, 72-84; and Kidco, Inc. (Elk Grove Village, IL) 1981-82.

T6800 TOWELS

Disney character towels have been made of linen, cotton and terry cloth. Smith, Hogg and Co. sold the largest line in the 30's made by several different manufacturers. Snow White linen hand towels are interesting for art on their paper tags, as well as their embroidery designs. Franco Mfg. Co. has turned out many great designs. (1976-84). Collector interest isn't high for any fabric products, but older towels bring 5 - 45. Some of the recent designs can cost 2 - 15 new, but value fades with each washing.

Licensed manufacturers — Luis Bergnes (NYC) 1949-50; Franco Mfg. Co., Inc. (NYC) 1976-84; Friedberger-Aaron Mfg. Co. (Philadelphia, PA) 1933-34; Gildex Corp. (NYC) 1951-53; Martex division of Wellington Sears Co. via Smith, Hogg & Co., Inc. (NYC) 1935-37; Printowel Corp. (NYC) 1938-40; and Wamsutta Mills, Inc. via M. Lowenstein & Sons (NYC) 1968.

T6407	F6060	F6061	T6405

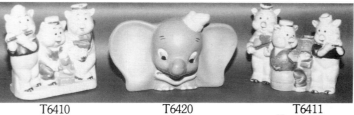

T6410	T6420	T6411

T6900 TOY CHESTS

Odora Co. made wood reinforced corrugated board toy chests from 1933-40. Fleischman produced wood designs 1944-46 and Gerston Brothers made masonite fiberboard units in the mid-50's. An unmarked litho metal "Toy Tub" was made in the late 60's or early 70's.

T6910 Mickey or Snow White (Odora) each	20 - 85
T6930 Mickey Mouse Club or Snow White (Gersten) each	10 - 35
T6945 Toy Tub	8 - 28
T6950 Corrugated storage chest (Mead)	3 - 12

Licensed manufacturers — Deka Plastics, Inc. (Elizabeth, NJ) 1984; Deluxe Game Corp. (Wilkes Barre, PA) 1968; Fleischman Mfg. Co. (NYC) 1944-46; Gerston Brothers, Inc. (NYC) 1953-54; Mead Containers (Cincinnati, OH) 1972-82; and Odora Company, Inc. (NYC) 1933.

T7900 TOYS — BATTERY OPERATED

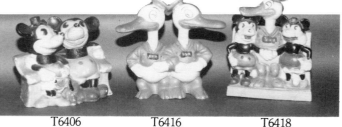

T6406	T6416	T6418

T6910

T6945

T6910

T7900

T6930

T8522

R6004

MECHANICAL

The most collectible Disney battery operated toys are the largely metal ones made in this country and Japan from the 50's to mid-60's. This, unfortunately, is the period where available records are sparse. Due to the relatively recent vintage, trading activity and toy availability information is also inconclusive. The major pieces known are a Mickey drummer, a similar Mickey magician, a walking Pluto and a character fire department ladder truck. These sell in the 55 - 275 range. Plastic and litho metal toys date to the late 60's or early 70's. Examples like the talking tourist bus (1966) bring 40 - 85. All plastic toys from 1970 to present range from 5 - 35. Batteries were used in toys found at many other classifications. Licensed manufacturers include — Frankonia Products, Inc. (NYC) 1966-68; General Molds & Plastics Corp. (Pittsburgh, PA); Gordy International, Inc. (East Brunswick, NJ) 1980-81; Illfelder Toy Co., Inc. (NYC) 1973-82; and Intoport Development Co., Inc. (Hong Kong) 1970's.

Also see TRAINS AND HANDCARS

T8500 TOYS — WOOD

George Borgfeldt & Co. sold many early wood figures and toys listed at this and other classifications. Toy Kraft made wood sand pails and pull toys. Bert B. Barry, a maker of Pinocchio wooden toys was one of the most curious of all licensees. The company paid to reproduce the Disney character, but instead continued to make Pinocchio toys of the company's design and mark them as being copyrighted by Walt Disney Productions. Fisher-Price was the largest producer of wood toys other than blocks. World War II material shortages prompted some interesting uses of wood. Strombecker wooden toys were made until 1959.

T8510	Toy Kraft wood sand pails	10 - 35
T8522	Pinocchio bus, plane or play room (Barry)	10 - 60
T8530	Flocked Mickey, Donald, Joe Carioca or Dumbo (Aime Des Biens), each	8 - 30
T8540	Timely Toys Mickey/Pluto, Donald or small Goofy, each	10 - 50
T8550	Strombecker wood toys, each	8 - 30

Licensed manufacturers — Aime Des Biens (Monterey Park, CA) 1944-45; Balantyne Supply Co. (Chicago) 1944-45, wood toys and carved figures; Bert B. Barry (Chicago) 1939-40, 48-49; George Borgfeldt & Co. (NYC) 1931-41; Strombeck-Becker Mfg. Co. (Moline, IL) 1955-59; Timely Toys (Chicago) 1945-46; and The Toy Kraft Co. (Wooster, OH) 1933-37.

Also see BLOCKS, DOLLS, FIGURES — WOOD, FISHER-PRICE, and ROCKING HORSES

T7900

T7900

T7900

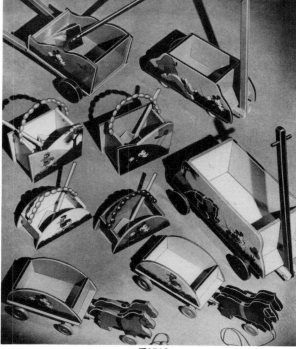

T8510

T8540

T9007

T9005

T9015

T9025

T9000 TRAINS AND HANDCARS

The Lionel Corporation was on the brink of bankruptcy when it acquired a license to make Mickey/Minnie handcars on July 19, 1934; a little over two months after going into receivership. On the strength of the license, it was permitted to borrow additional short term money. The loan was paid back two months early and the company was returned to its management on Jan 21, 1935 after repaying all its creditors. The headline on the Kay Kamen ad reproducing some of the many newspaper articles on the subject read "Red to Black on a Handcar — Mickey Mouse Pulls That Way". The Circus train and Santa handcar were added in 1935; other handcars in 1936. Louis Marx and Mar-Line made several trains and a Mickey/Donald handcar. Pride Lines, Ltd. hand crafted a streetcar for the tenth anniversary of Walt Disney World in 1981 and has originated and reproduced many rail pieces since.

The Lionel Corporation (T9005-T9020)

T9005	Mickey/Minnie handcar (Color variations exist)	175 - 450
T9006	Santa/Mickey handcar	200 - 500
T9007	Mickey Mouse Circus Train set, complete	2000 - 5000
T9008	Same as 9007, but train only	500 - 1500
T9010	Mickey freight or passenger train, each	150 - 400
T9015	Donald/Pluto handcar	200 - 500
T9020	Bi-Centennial train (Diesel locomotive, Caboose & 13 character box cars)	300 - 500
T9025	Mickey Mouse Meteor (Mar-Lines)	150 - 350
T9027	Mickey Mouse train on base (Marx)	75 - 200
T9028	Disneyville train set with cardboard accessories	100 - 275
	Mickey Mouse Express (see WIND-UP TOYS)	
T9030	Mickey/Donald handcar and base (Marx)	130 - 400
T9031	Same as T9030, handcar only	25 - 85
T9045	Disneyland train (metal locomotive) Marx	8 - 35
T9046	Casey Jr. Disneyland train (plastic locomotive) Marx	5 - 25

Pride Lines, Ltd. has produced many electric motorized street-cars and handcars. They are listed here with the original retail

T9010

T9006

T9031

T9030

T9025

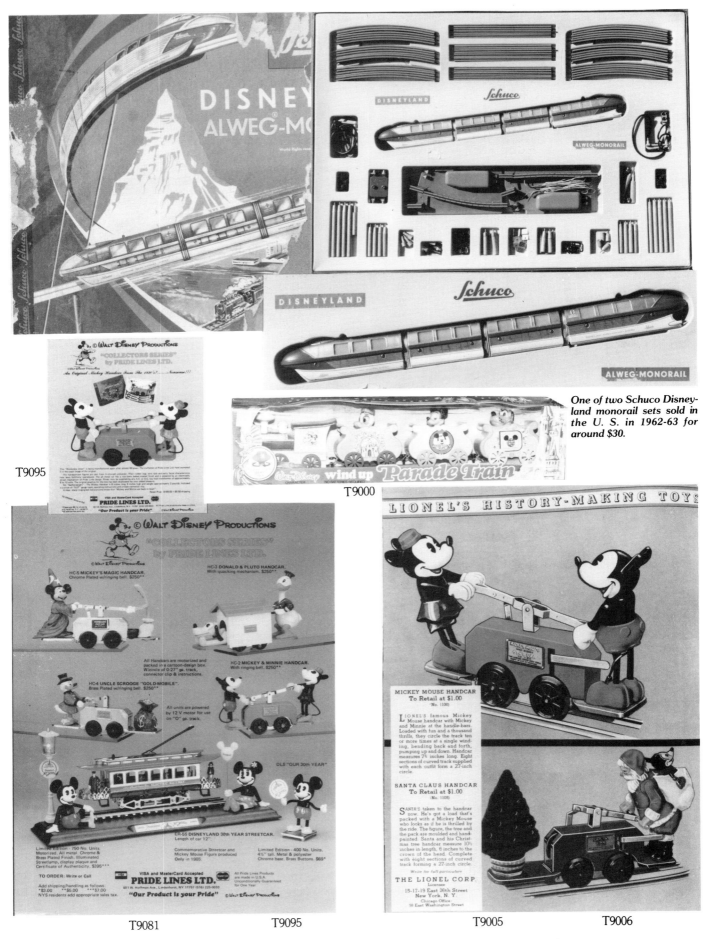

T9095

One of two Schuco Disneyland monorail sets sold in the U. S. in 1962-63 for around $30.

T9000

T9081   T9095

T9005   T9006

price for each unit.

T9081 Streetcars — Walt Disney World Tencennial ($275), Minnie Mouse — green ($275), Minnie Mouse — ivory ($275), Mickey Mouse — orange ($275), Donald's 50th Birthday — limited to 1,000 ($350) and Disneyland 30th Year — limited to 750 ($395).

T9095 Handcars — Mickey/Minnie Lionel repro ($250), Donald/Pluto Lionel repro ($250), Mickey Fantasia ($250), Uncle Scrooge "Gold Mobile" ($250) and Donald's 50th Birthday — limited to 1,000 ($295).

Licensed manufacturers — Durham Industries (NYC) 1972-83, battery operated trains; General Mills Fun Group, Inc. (see Lionel); The Lionel Corp. (NYC) 1934-38, and as a division of General Mills Fun Group, Inc. (Mt. Clemens, MI) 1972-80; Louis Marx & Co. also Mar-Lines and Line-Mar (NYC) 1936-80; Pines of America, Inc. (Ft. Wayne, IN) 1982-83, battery-operated train sets and ride-on trains; and Pride Lines Ltd. (Lindenhurst, NY) 1981-85.

T9200 TRAYS

Helen Hughes Dulany made trays (1933-35), Owens-Illinois Can Co. made a Snow White, and there were some 50's makers. Seen most often are the serving and bed trays made since 1960. Trays have proven to be popular theme park souvenirs.

T9201	Mickey trays from 30's	40 - 100
T9205	Snow White (Owens-Illinois)	30 - 90
T9220	Trays from 50's or 60's	2 - 12
T9250	Trays, 70's or 80's	1 - 6

Licensed manufacturers — California Metalware Corp. (El Segundo, CA) 1955-62; J. Chein & Co., Inc. (Newark, NJ) 1972-84; Helen Hughes Dulany (Chicago) 1933-35; Hasko Trays, Inc. (Indianapolis, IN) 1955-56; and MarshAllan Mfg. Co. (Cleveland, OH) 1979-83.

T9081

T9220

T9250

T9250

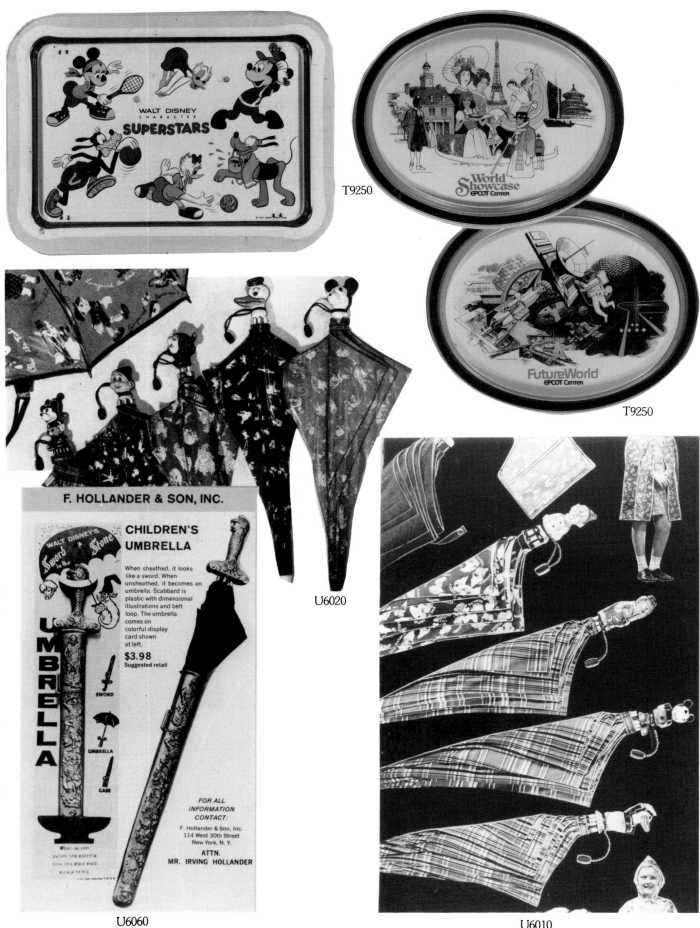

WALT DISNEY CHARACTER SUPERSTARS

T9250

World Showcase EPCOT Center

T9250

FutureWorld EPCOT Center

U6020

F. HOLLANDER & SON, INC.

WALT DISNEY'S Sword in the Stone

UMBRELLA

CHILDREN'S UMBRELLA

When sheathed, it looks like a sword. When unsheathed, it becomes an umbrella. Scabbard is plastic with dimensional illustrations and belt loop. The umbrella comes on colorful display card shown at left.

SWORD

UMBRELLA

CASE

$3.98
Suggested retail

FOR ALL INFORMATION CONTACT:

F. Hollander & Son, Inc.
114 West 30th Street
New York, N. Y.

ATTN.
MR. IRVING HOLLANDER

U6060

U6010

118

U6000 UMBRELLAS

George Borgfeldt (NYC) imported the first umbrellas from Japan, but Louis Weiss (NYC) took over in 1933 and produced Disney character umbrellas for over 25 years (1933-58). The Weiss products were sold in Canada by the W. A. Brophey Co., Ltd. F. Hollander & Son, Inc. (NYC) got the umbrella license sometime before 1963 and continued for over 20 years.

U6003	Mickey/Minnie ©Walter E. Disney (Borgfeldt)	45 - 110
U6005	Donald Duck ©Walt Disney Enterprises (Borgfeldt)	35 - 95
U6010	Weiss, 30's with full figure composition handle, each	18 - 60
U6020	Weiss, 40's with character head handle, each	15 - 45
U6040	Weiss, 50's	5 - 20
U6060	Sword in the Stone with scabbard cover	8 - 20
U6080	Umbrellas of the 60's, 70's and 80's	4 - 10

V1500 VALENTINES

Paper Novelty Manufacturing Co. produced some spectacularly printed valentines from 1938-42, many of them mechanical. They featured Snow White and the seven Dwarfs, Pinocchio and main characters. Little can be said for the cheap quality of Disney school valentine packs produced since the 60's. Hallmark did some nice individual cards each year. A series of chocolate valentines first appeared in the late 70's.

V1525	Snow White or Pinocchio regular Valentines, each	1 - 10
V1526	Snow White or Pinocchio small mechanical	2 - 15
V1527	Snow White or Pinocchio large mechanical	5 - 30
V1528	Main characters, regular	2 - 12
V1529	Main characters, mechanical	3 - 20

U6020

U6040

V1545　　　　V1525

V1526　　　　V1525　　　　V1527

V1529

V1526　　　　V1527

V1545

V1590

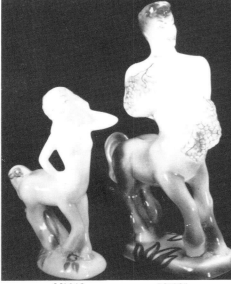

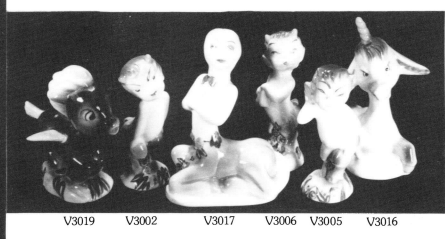

V3019   V3002   V3017   V3006 V3005   V3016

V3018   V3031

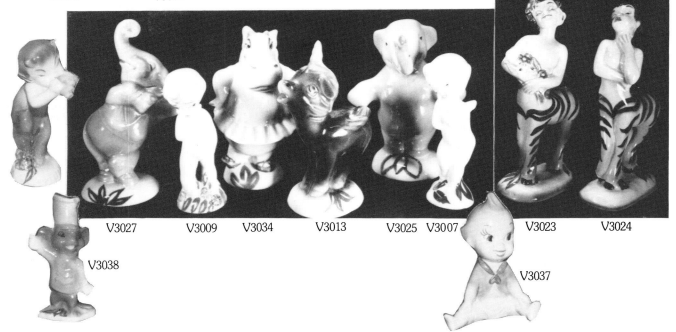

V3027   V3009   V3034   V3013   V3025 V3007   V3023   V3024

V3038

V3037

120

V1545	School assortment boxes (Fuld)	1 - 8
V1570	Hallmark individual cards, each	1 - 6
V1590	Chocolate Valentines (Kinnerton)	1 - 4

Licensed manufacturers — Colourpicture Publishers (Boston) 1979-84; Fuld & Company (Rockaway, NJ) then a division of Metropolitan Greetings, Inc. (Cambridge, MA) 1964-79; Hallmark Cards, Inc. (Kansas City, MO) 1972-84; Kinnerton Confectionary Co. (London and Long Island City, NY) imported 1979-82, U. S. 1983-84; and Paper Novelty Mfg. Co. (Brooklyn, NY) 1938-42.

V3000 VERNON KILNS CERAMICS

Vernon Potteries, Ltd. (LA) was a Disney licensee from Oct 10, 1940 to July 22, 1942 when they assigned all rights, inventory, and molds to American Pottery Company. In that short time the company distinguished itself as a major contributor to Disneyana. Thirty-six of the forty-two figurines, all eight bowls and vases, plus all the company's Disney china patterns were based on *Fantasia*. Molds for the figurines were made from models the animators used in creating the film. The figures are museum quality art. They provide collectors with a rare chance to own something close to the production models used in the making of all Disney animated features. Each figure has a number incised in the unglazed cavity, plus ink markings — "Disney Copyright 1940 (or 41) Vernon Kilns U. S. A." The last digit(s) in the Tomart number is (are) identical to the number incised on Vernon Kilns figures, bowls and vases. Some information and photos used in this section were supplied from the collection of Stan Pawlowski.

Valentine books. Value 1 - 10.

V1545

V3001-V3006	Satyrs, 4-1/2", each different	50 - 130
V3007-V3012	Sprites, standing, each different	45 - 135
V3008	Reclining Sprite	60 - 180
V3013	Unicorn, black with yellow horn	70 - 165
V3014	Sitting Unicorn, 5"	100 - 220
V3015	Rearing Unicorn, 6"	100 - 230
V3016	Donkey Unicorn, 5-1/2"	125 - 270
V3017	Reclining Centaurette, 5-1/2"	110 - 240
V3018	Centaurette, 7-1/2"	150 - 300
V3019	Baby Pegasus, black, 4-1/2"	60 - 175
V3020	White Pegasus, head turned, 5"	60 - 175
V3021	White Pegasus, 5-1/2"	60 - 175
V3022	Centaurette, 8-1/2"	125 - 350
V3023	Nubian Centaurette, 8"	150 - 375
V3024	Nubian Centaurette, 7-1/2"	150 - 375
V3025	Elephant, 5"	140 - 245
V3026	Elephant, trunk raised	150 - 280
V3027	Elephant, dancing, 5-1/2"	150 - 260
V3028	Ostrich, 6"	175 - 350
V3029	Ostrich, 8"	175 - 350
V3030	Ostrich, 9"	195 - 400
V3031	Centaur, 10"	450 - 650
V3032	Hippo, arm outstretched, 5-1/2"	140 - 245
V3033	Hippo	100 - 225
V3034	Hippo, 5"	100 - 225
V3035-36	Hop Low mushroom, salt and pepper set	75 - 100
V3037	Baby Weems	110 - 300
V3038	Timothy Mouse	75 - 125
V3039	Crow	175 - 300
V3040	Dumbo, falling on his ear	20 - 50
V3041	Dumbo, standing	45 - 85
V3042	Mr. Stork	175 - 350

(Higher values on bowls and vases are for hand painted rather than solid colors)

V3120	Mushroom bowl	35 - 125
V3121	Goldfish bowl	70 - 200
V3122	Winged Nymph bowl	45 - 150
V3123	Winged Nymph vase	100 - 185
V3124	Satyr bowl	75 - 135
V3125	Sprite bowl	90 - 155
V3126	Goddess vase	100 - 210
V3127	Pegasus vase	110 - 225

There were two basic designs to Vernon Kilns china dinnerware plate patterns — a border and a full plate design. The teapot, cream and sugar and salt and pepper are particularly attractive pieces in the set. Asking prices on dinnerware are 30 - 50 per large plate up to several hundred for a teapot, cream and sugar set in the most sought after patterns. The author has first hand knowledge of only one dinnerware sale — four dinner plates for 30 each.

V3122

V3500 VIDEO TAPES AND DISCS

The video revolution is scarcely upon us, but already several collectible items have resulted. Early video tapes were promoted in special premium packaging that included, at various times, stuffed Mickey, a special Christmas ornament and a birthday party kit. There were seven "Limited Gold Edition" tapes — each a collection of cartoons featuring the titled subject — Mickey, Donald, Pluto, Minnie, Daisy, Silly Symphonies, and Disney's Best: the Fabulous 50's. RCA Select-a-Vision CED video discs, along with several Disney titles in the format, have been discontinued. The first DiscoVision laser video disc programs featuring Mickey, Donald, and a 60's Wonderful World of Color program titled "Kids is Kids" have also been withdrawn. A Limited Gold Edition II has been released on both tape and laserdisc. The seven titles were: "Life with Mickey!", "An Officer and a Duck", "Donald's Bee Pictures", "From Pluto with Love", "The World According to Goofy", "The Disney Dream Factory: 1933-1938" and "How the Best Was Won: 1933-1960". A number of the animated features, including Pinocchio, have also been released. The retail price on Disney video products has ranged from $9.95 for the original DiscoVision programs to $79.95 for animated features on 1/2" tape formats. The median price has been around $35. Collector values will be established some time in the future when these packages are viewed similarly to the way we look at 78rpm records.

W0500 WALKING TOYS

Walkers in this class are not mechanical. They merely are balanced on moveable feet and waddle down an inclined plane. There were wood character walkers in the 40's, but the series of 14

W1035

W1035

V3500

V3500

W1045

W1018   W1019

W1045

Marx plastic walkers from the 50's were creatively done and have attracted collector interest. The different designs are: Pluto figural (a miniature version of the design exists), Donald and Goofy on bobsled, Jiminy Cricket pushing string bass on a wheel, Donald with wheelbarrel, Mickey and Minnie carrying basket of fruit, Big Bad Wolf and Practical Pig, Pluto and Mickey hunting, Goofy on Hippo, Minnie pushing baby buggy, 2 Pigs on hike, Mad Hatter and White Rabbit, Mickey and Donald on an alligator, Donald pushing lawn roller. Value 4 - 10 each. Earlier wooden walkers 6 - 45.

W1000 WALL DECORATION

Disney characters decorating a child's bedroom wall was such a natural combination. At least one licensee has produced a product in this category every year since Kerk Guild, Inc. offered the Mickey Mouse Art Gallery in 1936. The Dolly Toy Company has made die-cut multi-piece paper board scenes since 1951. Art prints, cels, framed pictures, and other Disneyana have also been used for this purpose.

W1010 Mickey Mouse Art Gallery (Kerk Guild), wooden figures with comic strip balloon, boxed set of 1 or 2 figures	25 - 75
W1011 Individual figures, Mickey, Minnie, Pluto, Clara or Donald, each	8 - 20
W1012 Individual pieces, 1938-51, each	5 - 15
W1018 Artisto "framed" pictures (no glass), Snow White, Dwarfs, each	5 - 20
W1019 Mickey, Minnie, Donald or Pluto (1938), each	10 - 30
W1035 Dimensional coloring plaque kits, Mickey, Donald, Pluto, Bambi, Flower, or Thumper (1942), Youngstown Pressed Steel, each	5 - 15
W1045 Fuzzy wall plaques (Plane Facts) set	10 - 30
W1050 Cinderella 3-dimensional scenes (Wessel)	10 - 25
W1054 Alice in Wonderland and Pinocchio, cloth on cardboard, each	4 - 9
W1060 Dolly Toy Company scenes, Cinderella, Casey Jr., Donald and Nephews, Snow White and 7 Dwarfs, Pinocchio, Mickey Mouse Clubhouse, Bambi or Winnie the Pooh, normally 4 pieces per scene, each	3 - 12
W1075 Snow White and Seven Dwarfs embroidered pictures (E.P.I.C.), set	10 - 35
W1085 Disney panorama wall mural, 65" x 45" (Glenview)	10 - 25
W1090 Classic Disney scenes on masonite (Priss Prints), each	2 - 4
W1120 Embossed wood-like character frames, 5 different, sold new at theme parks, © 1982-84, each	10 - 20

W0500

W1010

W1060

W1012

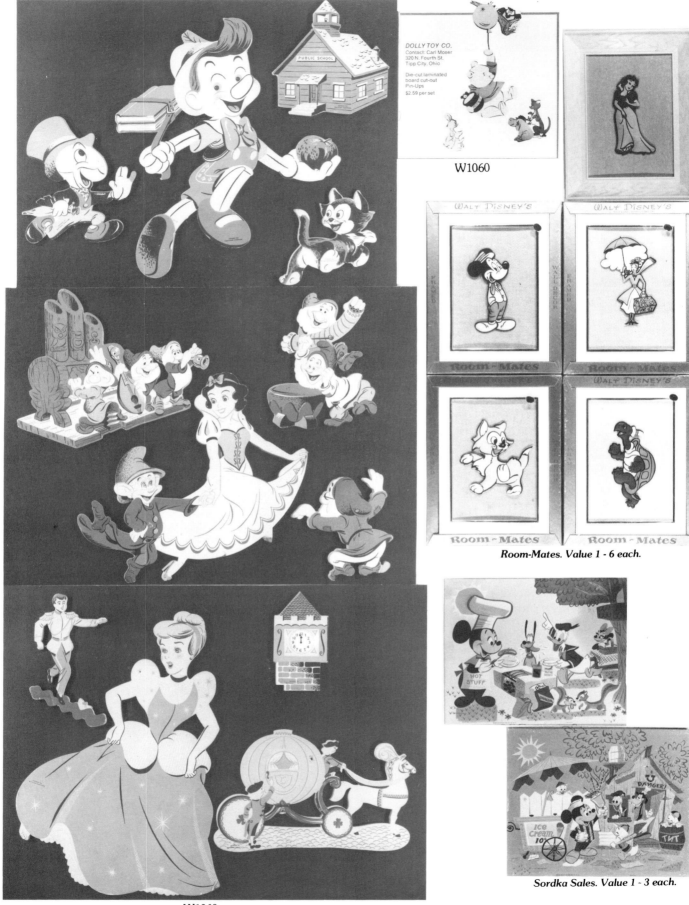

DOLLY TOY CO.
Contact: Carl Moser
320 N. Fourth St.
Tipp City, Ohio

Die-cut laminated
board cut-out
Pin-Ups
$2.59 per set

W1060

Room-Mates. Value 1 - 6 each.

Sordka Sales. Value 1 - 3 each.

W1060

Licensed manufacturers — Artisto, Inc. (NYC) 1938-39; Bradford Novelty Co. Inc. (Cambridge, MA) 1955-56, Mickey Mouse Club wall plaques; Chicago Superior Mirror Works (Chicago) 1944-46; Continental Paper Box Company (Philadelphia, PA) 1970-73, framed character wall plaques; Decoplaque, Inc. (NYC) 1980, Christmas wall plaques; The Dolly Toy Co. (Dayton, then Tipp City, OH) 1951-84; E.P.I.C., Inc. (Philadelphia, PA) 1968; Fine Arts Pictures (NYC) 1937-39, cut-out figures and wall plaques; Fotoplak Co. (NYC) 1942-43; Glenview Products, Inc. — Moebius Printing (Milwaukee, WI) 1968; Kerk Guild, Inc. (NYC) 1936-39, 45-51; Norman Industries, Inc. (LA) 1970-74, polyester wall decorations; Pancordion, Inc. (NYC) 1953-55; Plane Facts, Inc. (NYC) 1943-45; Priss Prints, Inc. (Falls Mills, VA) 1975-84; Service Industries, Inc. (Chicago) 1937-38, masonite cut-outs; Soroka Sales, Inc. (Pittsburgh, PA) 50's and 60's; Stanley Wessel & Co. (Chicago) 1950-51; Youngstown Pressed Steel Co. unit of Mullins Mfg. Corp. (Warren, OH) 1942-43.

Also see ANIMATION CELS, MAPS, PRINTS — ART and POSTERS

W1500 WALLETS AND BILLFOLDS

Most of the licensees listed at PURSES also made wallets of leather, vinyl, nylon or other material. Additional manufacturers specifically licensed for products in this class are listed here. Value 1 - 15.

Licensed manufacturers — Aristocrat Leather Products, Inc. (NYC) 1955-64; Centia Leather Goods Corp. (NYC) 1948-49; Fox Sportswear, Inc. (San Marcos, CA) 1982; Kestral Corp. (Springfield, MA) 1953-54; and Salient, Inc. (Holyoke, MA) 1951-52.

W1054

W1050

Value 1 - 4 each.

E. P. I. C. inc., 925 N. Third St., Philadelphia, Pa. 19132 — Contact: Howard Sernaker

W1075

W1090

W1120

GLENVIEW PRODUCTS, INC.

DISNEY PANORAMA WALL MURAL

Famous Walt Disney cartoon characters, including Merlin, Wart and Archimedes, in full color on 65"x45" durable paper. #CM6503. $5.95 Suggested retail.

FOR ALL INFORMATION REGARDING THIS CROWN MURAL
CONTACT:
GLENVIEW PRODUCTS, INC. (Moebius Printing)
Attn. Mr. Howard Moebius
300 N. Jefferson, Milwaukee, Wis.

W1612

W1623

W1622

W1620

W1631

W1975

WALT DISNEY PRODUCTIONS **ANNUAL REPORT 1971**

Walt Disney Productions ANNUAL REPORT

W1700

W1911

W1970

W1971

W1600 WALLPAPER AND TRIM

United Wall Paper Factories introduced character wallpaper in 1935 and were a major source until 1950. The Trimz Company provided some typical late 40's designs. Cohn-Hall-Marx sold self-adhesive "con-tact" paper in 1968. Collectibles dealers often sheet out rolls or trim strips in segments of one complete pattern.

W1610 Dual roll, two 36″ repeating patterns (United), 1935, roll	25 - 75
W1611 Sheets from W1610	5 - 10
W1612 Design including long bill Donald, roll	30 - 90
W1613 Sheet from W1612	7 - 12
W1620 Trimz full rolls	12 - 30
W1621 Sheets from W1620	2 - 5
W1622 Trimz ceiling boarder dispenser	6 - 15
W1623 Sheet from W1622	1 - 3
W1630 Wallpaper rolls, other	1 - 15
W1631 Sheets from W1630	.50 - 2

Licensed manufacturers — Birge Wallcoverings (Buffalo, NY) 1980; Child Life Wallpaper Co., Inc. (Kingston, NY) 1953; Cohn-Hall-Marx Co. (NYC) 1968; Morgan Adhesives Co. (Stow, OH) 1970-74; Reed Holding, Inc. (Buffalo, NY) 1979, 81-82 (see Birge for 81); Trimz Co., Inc. (Chicago) 1947-48; and United Wall Paper Factories (Jersey City, NJ) 1935-37, 44-50, wallpaper boarders and strips.

W1700 WALT DISNEY PRODUCTIONS ANNUAL REPORTS

The framework of Walt Disney Productions as a publicly owned company was finalized in the fall of 1939. Annual reports have been issued each year beginning in 1940. Reports since 1968 sell for 1 - 10. Earlier ones 10 - 50. The 1940 report goes for 20 - 100.

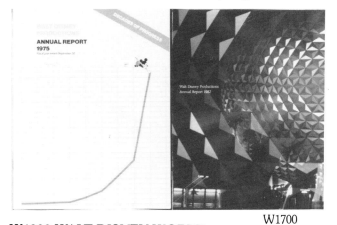

W1700

W1900 WALT DISNEY WORLD

"The Florida Project" was planned, designed, and implemented under tight security to avoid an onrush of land speculators like those who choked off Disneyland. On Oct 25, 1965, Walt Disney announced the company had purchased nearly 44 square miles of orange groves and swamp land near Orlando, Florida. Walt died a year later, but Walt Disney World opened as scheduled on Oct 1, 1971. On Oct 25, 1971, Roy Disney formally dedicated the new venture to his brother, the entire Disney organization, and all in the world who seek "a Magic Kingdom where the young at heart of all ages can laugh and play and learn — together." In the first 10 years over $750 million was spent on construction. In addition to the Magic Kingdom, the complex includes three Disney hotel resorts (the Contemporary, Polynesian and Golf Resort; the original plan also included the Asian, Persian and Venetian, yet to be built), Fort Wilderness Campgrounds, Discovery Island (a zoo, originally called Treasure Island), River Country swimming resort and the city of Lake Buena Vista with major hotels, shopping center, condominiums, "treehouses", offices, recreation and restaurants. EPCOT Center is also on the property, and a Disney/MGM Studio Tour has been announced for the future. Souvenirs and collectibles are everywhere and constantly changing. Even operating supplies are intriguing as they change from one promotion to the next. Much of the merchandise is listed at various classifications throughout this series. The items listed here are a small part of the items exclusively connected with the "World" and its operation.

W1610

W1700

W1700

W1905

W1960

W1981

W1984

W1990

D5060

W1915

W1978

W1960

W1940

W1985

128

W4110

W4130

W4110

W1992

W4172

W4160

W4155

W4207

W4224

W4204

W4203

W4205

Also see DISNEYLAND, EMPLOYEE PUBLICATIONS, EPCOT CENTER, PINBACK BUTTONS, and POSTCARDS

W4100 WASHING MACHINES AND WASH TUBS

Ohio Art made litho tin laundry sets (consisting of a wash tub, scrub board and clothes rack) for the Three Pigs and Mickey/Minnie (smaller). The company's litho tin washing machine reportedly did a nice job on doll clothes. Precision Specialties made plastic washing machines and Modere Toys made a Donald litho automatic washer.

W4110 Laundry sets, complete in box (Ohio Art)   40 - 120
W4111 Three Pigs tub and scrub board only   20 - 60
W4112 Mickey/Minnie tub and scrub board only   20 - 50
W4115 Litho tin washing machine (Ohio Art) 1935   30 - 110
W4125 Snow White or Minnie plastic washing machine
    (Precision)   15 - 45
W4130 Donald automatic washer   10 - 40
Licensed manufacturers — Modere Toys (made in Japan) c. 50's; Ohio Art Company (Bryan, OH) 1933-42, 44-45; and Precision Specialties, Inc. (LA) 1945-52.

W4150 WASTEBASKETS

Geuder, Paeschke & Frey Co. made two different main character wastebaskets in 1936. A cardboard basket featuring United Wall Paper Factories borders may have been commercial or homemade. Several modern designs incorporate the 30's Mickey style, but were made in the 70's and 80's.

W4155 Mickey's gang, 2 designs (1936), each   40 - 100
W4160 Cardboard wastebasket with wallpaper border   30 - 55
W4172 Cheinco (1972-84), each   1 - 6
Licensed manufacturers — Cheinco — J. Chein & Co., Inc. (NYC) 1972-84; E. S. G. Industries, Inc. (Elgin, IL) 1970-71; Geuder, Paeschke & Frey Co. (Milwaukee, WI) 1935-37; and Modern Woodworking Co. (Burbank, CA) 1957, redwood wastepaper baskets with Disneyland Art Corner decals.

W4200 WATCHES

The Ingersoll Waterbury Co., like Lionel Corp., was on the brink of the Depression disaster when they created the Mickey Mouse watch in 1933. Nearly 2 million watches were sold the first year. The company prospered with Mickey and today it is known by a new name, Timex Corp. There have been other names over the years and for a time there were no watches made with Mickey's image. Many other Disney characters have appeared on time pieces too. Often the same watch was packaged in different ways. In 1972, Elgin National Industries and subsequently its Bradley Time division (1976) acquired the license for Disney watches and clocks. Many early watches were made in England and other countries, but these were not officially sold in the U.S.

Ingersoll-Waterbury Company (W4003-W4030)
W4203 Mickey Mouse pocket watch   80 - 200
W4204 Mickey Mouse wrist watch-metal band   65 - 175
W4205 Mickey wrist watch-leather band with metal
    Mickeys   75 - 185
W4207 Sterling advertising fob   50 - 250
W4210 Three Pigs and Wolf pocket watch and fob   150 - 400
W4211 Three Pigs and Wolf wrist watch   75 - 200
W4217 Mickey lapel watch with decal on back   100 - 250
W4218 Same as W4005, Donald is main figure   150 - 350
W4224 Rectangular Mickey wrist watch with revolving
    Mickeys second hand   100 - 200
W4225 Same as W4024, but deluxe version with
    Mickey and Donald charms on band   150 - 250
W4226 Same as W4024, but regular second hand   50 - 135
W4230 Donald Duck pocket watch with Mickey decal
    on reverse   100 - 250

W4111   W4112   W4115

W4125

W4225   W4217

W4230

W4288

W4285

W4241   W4242

W4261

W4249   W4282

W4240

W4260

W4248   W4246

132

Ingersoll/U. S. Time (W4040-W4099)

W4240 Mickey, rectangular, pupil eyes (1946)	35 - 95
W4241 Donald, rectangular (1946)	60 - 150
W4242 Snow White or Daisy, rectangular	100 - 175
W4245 Mickey, head only (Kelton/U. S. Time)	75 - 150
W4246 Mickey, round, two sizes (1947)	20 - 80
W4248 Donald round, adult (1947)	30 - 90
W4249 In 1948 Ingersoll offered 10 different character watches with luminous hand dials. This 20th birthday watch promotion featured Mickey, Donald, Daisy, Pluto, Bongo, Pinocchio, Jiminy Cricket, Dopey, Joe Carioca and Bambi, each	20 - 65
W4260 Mickey's 20th birthday watch in cake box	100 - 200
W4261 In 1949 the same series was reoffered in special boxes that included a ball point pen with Mickey or Donald decal, boxed, each	55 - 125
W4275 Cinderella wrist watch	15 - 55
W4280 Davy Crockett wrist watch	15 - 55
W4282 Zorro wrist watch (Name only)	10 - 40
W4285 Cinderella, Snow White and Alice in Wonderland wrist watches with ceramic statuettes of namesake, with image on watch dial, each	20 - 55
W4288 Same as W4085, except figures are plastic and only name appears on watch	10 - 30
W4299 Mickey Mouse wrist watch, no image, name only	10 - 25
W4300 Mickey Mouse Timex electric (1970)	150 - 300

Elgin National Industries/Bradley Time (W4125-W4400)

Elgin and Bradley Time continued innovative packaging and added a lot of product excitement by reintroducing pocket watches, pendant and lapel watches, animated and digital wrist watches, plus special edition watches. The number of different watches produced since 1972 far exceed the number of Ingersol/U. S. Time/Timex watches produced from 1933-1971. These are categorized rather than identified by individual watch.

W4325 Child's character wrist watch, regular	15 - 30
W4350 Special event wrist watch	20 - 50
W4375 Regular and Railroad pocket watches, each	15 - 40
W4390 Special event pocket watches, each	25 - 100
W4400 Numbered special editions, each	20 - 60
W4425 Same as W4200, but precious metal, each	50 - 250
W4500 Animated children's wrist watches, each	20 - 50
W4600 Children's plastic play watches, each	1 - 4

Licensed manufacturers — Elgin National Industries (NYC) 1972-77 and Bradley Time Division (NYC) 1976-84; Ingersoll-Waterbury Co. (Waterbury, CT) 1933-44 succeeded by United States Time Corp. (NYC) 1945-69 with name revision to Timex Corp. (NYC) 1970-71; and G. R. L'Esperance (Canadian) 1949-50.

W6300 WATER GUNS

Plastic figural water guns were made in the 50's. Value 2 - 15. Head only versions, also plastic, were made in the 70's. Value 1 - 3.

W6400 WEATHER HOUSES AND VANES

The Weatherman (Chicago) 1946-53 made a plastic weather forecaster valued at 10 - 40. Always be sure the blue rooster is on top before buying. A plastic wind direction, rain and temperature unit was sold in the 70's — value 1 - 5.

W6500 WHEEL GOODS — BICYCLES, WAGONS, SCOOTERS, ETC.

Bikes, wagons and similar products are difficult collectibles in a small home or apartment. Yet the Colson Mickey Mouse velocipede (tricycle) that Mickey "helped" pedal and the Shelby Donald Duck boys' two-wheeler would tempt even the most cramped collector. Other types of wheel goods are listed below. The Davy Crockett "Western Prairie Wagon" is more doll sized and has attractive litho tin front and sides.

W6503 Mickey Mouse velocipede (tricycle)	80 - 375
W6510 Mickey/Minnie 23" wagon (Dayton)	35 - 150
W6511 Mickey Mouse 10" wagon (Dayton)	35 - 150
W6512 Wheelbarrow, two sizes (Dayton), each	30 - 100
W6515 Pedal car (trike) or scooter (Dayton)	30 - 90
W6530 Donald Duck 16" or 20" bike (Shelby)	45 - 200
W6545 Davy Crockett wagons (Liberty National)	25 - 70
W6550 Mouseketeer wagons or scooter (Radio Flyer)	20 - 65

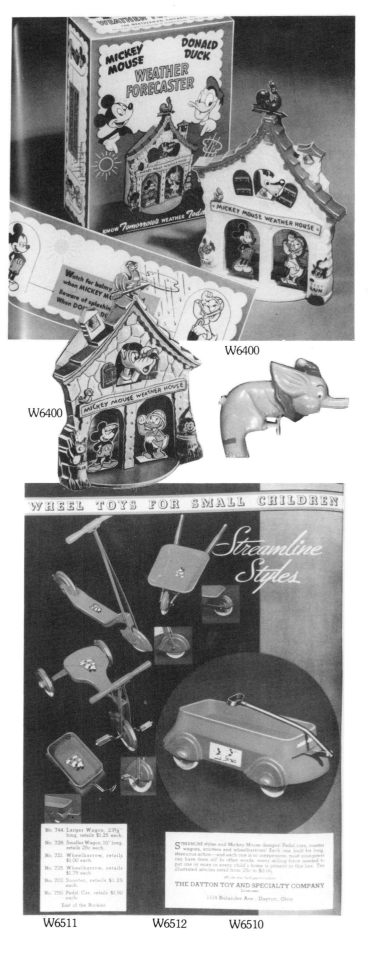

W6400

W6400

W6511   W6512   W6510

133

W6503

W6530

W7120

W7144

W7039

W7115

See Mouseketeer Wagons and Scooter at your neighborhood department, hardware or toy store.

W6550

W7045

Licensed maufacturers — Ad-Vance Trailer Corp. (NYC) 1931, trailers; The Colson Co. (Elyria, OH) 1933-35; The Dayton Toy and Specialty Co. (Dayton, OH) 1935-36; Intercontinent Toy Corp. (NYC) 1945-46, tricycles and bicycles; Liberty National Corp. (NYC) 1954-56; Pines of America, Inc. (Ft. Wayne, IN) 1982-83, battery operated ride-on train and pedal drive "Pine Mobile"; Radio Steel & Mfg. Co. — Radio Flyer (Chicago) 1956-59; Shelby Cycle Co. (Shelby, OH) 1949-50; and Stebber Cycle Corp. (Elmhurst, NY) 1968, tricycles.

W7000 WIND-UP TOYS

Wind-up toys combine art and engineering to provoke curiosity and fascination. They are as intriguing today as they were the day they were removed from the original box. Values are naturally higher if the toy is in good working condition. Some of the earliest Disney wind-up toys were made of celluloid in Japan and imported by George Borgfeldt & Co. There were undetermined variations of these delicate toys made until 1942. There were also celluloid toys made after the War, but these had pupil rather than pie-cut eyes. The same company imported Schuco wind-ups from Germany around 1932-37. Louis Marx introduced U. S. made litho tin toys in late 1937 and made wind-ups (some plastic) until the 50's. In the late 40's, however, Marx added litho tin wind-ups made in Japan under the name Linemar. Other makers made plastic or tin wind-ups till the mid-50's. Linemar litho tin wind-ups were made until 1961 at least. Small plastic wind-up figures made by TOMY (Japan) began turning up as theme park souvenirs around 1978. Five fingered Mickey with teeth litho tin wind-ups by English and German makers (c. 1929-31) W7002-W7020

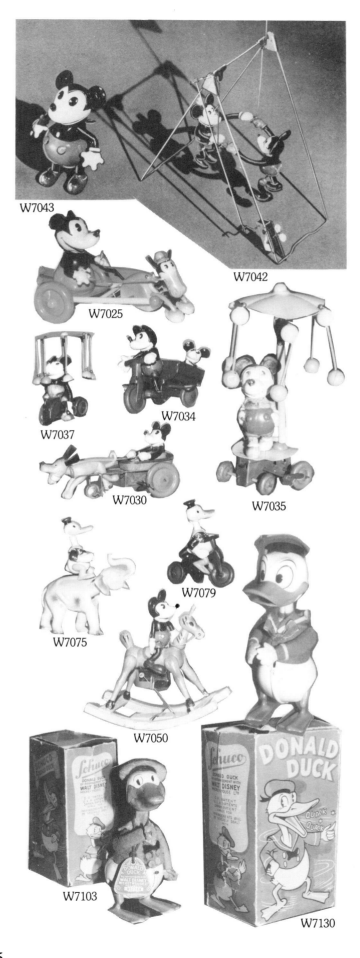

W7043
W7042
W7025
W7034
W7037
W7030
W7035
W7079
W7075
W7050
W7103
W7130

W7002 Mickey Mouse Slate Dancer	500 - 2500
W7004 Mickey and Minnie on motorcycle	2500 - 5000
W7005 Mickey Mouse Musical Band	1000 - 3800
W7007 Mickey walker	1000 - 4000
W7008 Mickey walker with moving eyes	3000 - 11000
W7010 Mickey and Minnie organ grinder	1500 - 4000
W7012 Mickey Mouse paddle boat	800 - 3000
W7014 Minnie pushing Felix the Cat in carriage	2500 - 5000
W7015 Mickey Mouse with Felix the Cat in basket	1000 - 3000
W7017 Mickey and Felix lighting cigars	2000 - 4500
W7020 Mickey Mouse drummer	500 - 1000

Celluloid Wind-ups made in Japan (W7025-W7085)

W7025 Horace Horsecollar pulling Mickey	2500-5000
W7028 Mickey on celluloid Pluto with wooden rockers	600 - 1400
W7030 Pluto pulling Mickey in cart	250 - 700
W7031 Mickey walking Pluto	275 - 750
W7034 Mickey driving 3-wheel cart with mouse	275 - 750
W7035 Standing Mickey whirligig	300 - 800
W7037 Mickey tricycle whirligig	250 - 650
W7038 Mickey on tricycle	150 - 350
W7039 Mickey trapeze I	125 - 275
W7040 Mickey trapeze II	75 - 200
W7042 Mickey/Minnie swing (facing each other)	75 - 200
W7043 Mickey walker, 6"	300 - 500
W7045 Three Pigs trapeze	100 - 300
W7046 Mickey/Minnie trapeze (both to front)	90 - 250
W7047 Balloon man with toys (one is Mickey)	125 - 250
W7050 Mickey on wooden rocking horse	450 - 900
W7052 Mickey whirligig with dangle characters	450 - 900
W7070 Long bill Donald walker, 4-1/2"	175 - 350
W7071 Long bill Donald walker, 3"	150 - 300
W7074 Mickey and Donald trapeze	125 - 275
W7075 Long bill Donald on elephant	425 - 850
W7078 Pluto pulling long bill Donald in cart	200 - 650
W7079 Long bill Donald on tricycle	135 - 325
W7082 Long bill Donald whirligig	250 - 675
W7085 Long bill Donald whirligig with characters	275 - 750
W7100 Tumbling Mickey (Schuco)	100 - 250
W7102 Three Pigs playing fife, fiddle or drum (Schuco), each	100 - 250
W7103 Walking-squawking long bill Donald (Schuco), 1st version, all metal	300 - 800
W7110 Mickey Mouse Speedway Car, complete set	250 - 800
W7111 Individual Mickey or Donald cars for W7110, each	35 - 150
W7115 Composition Donald walker (Borgfeldt) 1938	125 - 275
W7118 Dopey walker (Marx) 1938	50 - 145
W7119 Ferdinand the Bull (Marx) 1939	45 - 95

W7122

W7123

W7180

W7189

W7135

W7146

W7248

W7125   W7124   W7133

T9027

T9028

W7161   W7162   W7160

136

W7120 Composition Pinocchio walker (Borgfeldt)   125 - 275
W7122 Pinocchio walker (Marx) 1939   55 - 145
W7123 Pinocchio the Acrobat 1939   60 - 160
W7124 Wise Pluto (Marx) 1940   35 - 60
W7125 Roll Over Pluto (Marx) 1940   40 - 75
W7126 Roll Over Figaro (Marx) 1941   45 - 85
W7127 Bouncing Dumbo (Marx) 1941   50 - 150
W7130 Donald Duck with plastic bill (Schuco)   175 - 250
W7133 Tail wind Pluto (Marx)   45 - 85
W7134 Goofy the Gardener (Marx)   135 - 275
W7135 Donald Duck (and Goofy) Duet (Marx) 1946   100 - 225
W7136 Mickey Mouse Express (Marx) 1949   150 - 350
W7138 Mickey, Donald or Pluto Gym Toy Acrobat,
     celluloid figures with pupil eyes
     (Linemar), each   125 - 185
W7141 Walt Disney's Rocking Chair, Celluloid Donald
     with pupil eyes on litho tin Dumbo rocker
     activated by pulling string anchored by solid
     plastic Pluto (Linemar)   150 - 285
W7144 Merry-go-round with 4 celluloid figures   125 - 200
W7145 Disney Parade Roadster (Marx)   95 - 235
W7146 Pecos Bill Ridin' Widowmaker (Marx), plastic   75 - 175
W7148 Donald Duck and his nephews (Marx), plastic   125 - 250
W7149 Donald the Skier (Marx), plastic   125 - 250
W7150 Donald the Drummer (Marx), plastic with metal
     drum, 2 sizes   55 - 225
W7160 Donald Duck (Mavco)   65 - 135
W7161 Donald Duck the Gay Caballero (Mavco)   65 - 135
W7162 Mickey Mouse Scooter Jockey (Mavco)   75 - 135
W7165 Mickey the Musician (xylophone), no note came
     in the center (Marx), plastic   65 - 135
W7170 Fuzzy walking Donald   65 - 155
W7175 Mickey with rotating wire tail, plastic (Marx)   30 - 65
W7176 Pluto with rotating wire tail, plastic (Marx)   25 - 50
W7178 Mickey with rotating wire tail, metal (Linemar)   35 - 75
W7180 Mickey's Disney jalopy (Linemar)   40 - 85
W7185 Dancing Cinderella and Prince (Irwin)   30 - 65
W7188 Mechanical Donald with rotating tail   35 - 75
W7189 Mechanical Goofy with rotating tail   35 - 75
W7190 Mechanical Pluto with rotating tail   35 - 75
W7191 Pluto pulling cart (Linemar)   75 - 150
W7192 Mickey riding rocking horse Pluto (Linemar)   85 - 165
W7194 Partying Pluto (Linemar)   55 - 120
W7195 Climbing Fireman Donald (Linemar)   75 - 155
W7200 Minnie on rocker knitting (Linemar)   90 - 195
W7204 Mickey, Pluto or Goofy on unicycle (Linemar),
     each   35 - 75
W7206 Big Bad Wolf jumper (Linemar)   60 - 165
W7207 Jumping Three Pigs (Linemar), each   50 - 115
W7214 Mickey or Donald crazy car (Linemar), metal
     figures, each   65 - 135
W7216 Mickey or Donald crazy car (Linemar), plastic
     figures, each   60 - 130
W7220 Donald drummer, metal (Linemar)   75 - 225
W7225 Remote squeeze action Donald, Pluto, Jiminy
     Cricket, or Bambi (Linemar), not wind-up, each   45 - 95
W7245 Disneyland Ferris Wheel (Chein)   70 - 175
W7246 Disneyland Roller coaster (Chein)   75 - 185

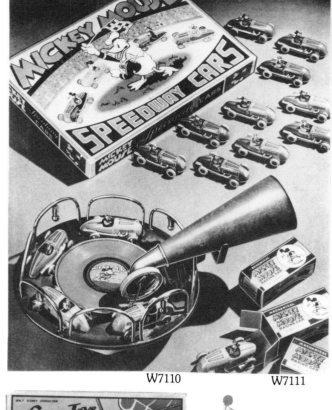

W7110   W7111

W7138

W7188

On skates. Value 75 - 300.
W7200

W7178

W7149

W7136

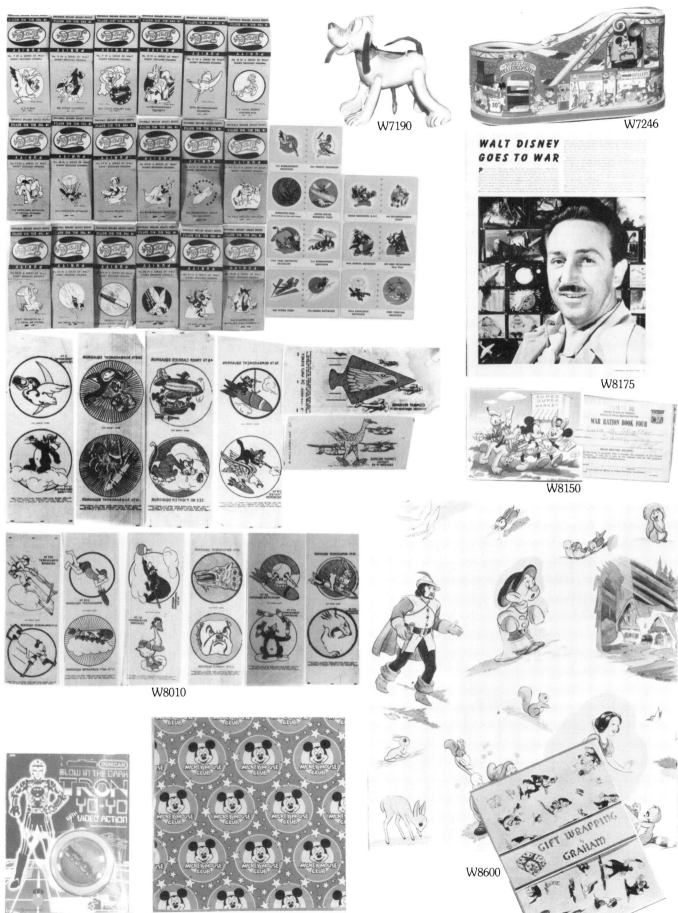

W7190

W7246

WALT DISNEY GOES TO WAR

W8175

W8150

W8010

W8600

Y5000

W8600

W8600

138

W7248 Pinocchio, Toy Soldier or Ludwig Von Drake
  walker (Linemar), 1961, each   35 - 95
Licensed manufacturers — George Borgfeldt & Co. (NYC) 1931-41; J. Chein & Co. Inc. (Newark, NJ) 1953-55; Charles William Doepke Mfg. Co., Inc. (Rossmayne, OH) 1955, Mickey Mouse Club express, outdoor train, and Disneyland copter; Irwin Corp. (Fitchburg, MA) 1949-51; Lesney Products Corp. (NYC) c.1971-72, wind-up mechanical vehicles; Louis Marx & Co. (NYC) 1936-61 (68-80 for non-wind-ups); Mavco, Inc. (NYC) 1947-51 (plastic toys, 1949-50); Joseph Schneider, Inc. (NYC) 1936-38; and Schuco (Germany) c. 1932-34, 48-56.

W8000 WORLD WAR II

The bombing of Pearl Harbor had an immediate and lasting impact on the newly formed Walt Disney Productions. Hundreds of soldiers took over part of the studio for preparations. Over 1,200 military insignias were designed gratis and regular projects were pushed aside to make training films. Cartoons and animated shorts took a new slant to support the war effort. Disney artists also designed uncounted posters, program covers for events, even holders for ration stamp books. Kids bought insignia iron-on transfers while their dads lit cigarettes with matches from Pepsi-Cola's matchbook cover series using many of the same Disney designs. There was even a trading card series. Magazine articles offer some good insight on what was going on at the studio during this period. A couple of special war publications were attempted, but were abandoned.

W8010 Insignia designs on transfers, matchbook covers,
  or trading cards, each item   1 - 6
W8050 Posters providing troop information, USO activities
  or a message for defense plant workers, each   5 - 50
W8100 Programs with war support art, each   10 - 45
W8150 Ration book holder   8 - 25
W8175 Magazine articles   2 - 10
W8200 House organs or other World War II items   1 - 75
Licensed manufacturers — Home Front Publishing Co. (NYC) and Pepsi-Cola or the matchbook company.

W8600 WRAPPING PAPER, RIBBON AND TAPE

Disney gift wrap was a natural tie-in to the warmth, happiness and entertainment Walt Disney was projecting in his films. General Graham Manufacturing was one of the earliest licensees in 1938 and, except for war shortage periods, the product has remained almost constantly available. These products are not big collector items, but bring 5 - 18 for older unused packages.
Licensed manufacturers — Buzza-Cardozo (Anaheim, CA) 1970-71; Chicago Printed String Co. (Chicago) 1939-42; Cleo Wrap Corp. (Memphis, TN) 1968-84; General Ribbon Mills, Inc. (NYC) 1933-36, 38-41; Graham Mfg. Co. (Holyoke, MA) 1938-39; Hallmark Cards, Inc. (Kansas City, MO) 1972-84; Industrial Tape Corp. (New Brunswick, NJ) 1944-50, gift tape and transfers; Leadworks, Inc. (Beachwood, OH) 1982-83, tape; Minnesota

W8050

W8100

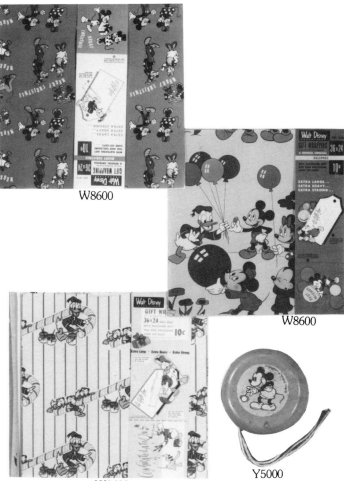

W8600

W8600

W8600

Y5000

W8600

Y5000

Z5015

Z5096

Z5011

Z5022

Z5060

D3060

Z5080

B3127

Z5020

Z5018

Z5035